THE HAIKU FORM

BY JOAN GIROUX

CHARLES E. TUTTLE COMPANY
RUTLAND • VERMONT | TOKYO • JAPAN

Representatives

For Continental Europe:
BOXERBOOKS, INC., Zurich

For the British Isles:
PRENTICE-HALL INTERNATIONAL, INC., London

For Australasia:
PAUL FLESCH & CO., PTY. LTD., Melbourne

For Canada:
HURTIG PUBLISHERS, Edmonton

Published by the Charles E. Tuttle Company, Inc.
of Rutland, Vermont & Tokyo, Japan
with editorial offices at
Suido 1-chome, 2-6, Bunkyo-ku, Tokyo

Library of Congress Catalog Card No. 73-86135
International Standard Book No. 0-8048 1110-5

First printing, 1974

PRINTED IN JAPAN

TABLE OF
CONTENTS

NOTE ON JAPANESE NAMES

All are given here in Japanese order, with the family name before the personal name. In the name Matsuo Basho, for example, Matsuo, the family name, is given first. In referring to famous writers, however, Japanese often use the personal name only; this practice has also been followed here in discussions of famous poets like Basho and Buson.

PREFACE

The haiku form was first discovered by English-speaking visitors to Japan about a hundred years ago. In the last twenty years, however—an era which has introduced pocket-sized transistor radios, miniskirts and fast foods—it is not surprising that there has been a resurgence of interest in a brief poetic form expressing an instant of insight. Interest in Zen Buddhism and the contacts with Eastern culture made by the Occupation troops and their families after World War II have contributed to an increased knowledge of haiku. Numerous haiku contests, articles in teachers' magazines, and even several "little magazines" and volumes of poetry devoted exclusively to haiku in English give witness to its popularity as a poetry form. In spite of the enthusiasm, however, it is doubtful whether the majority of these would-be writers of haiku really understand the meaning of haiku, the cultural climate which produces it and the technical difficulties stemming from the differences between Japanese and English.

It is the purpose of this book to examine the problems of writing haiku in English. Several excellent books and articles, it is true, have already been written about the Japanese haiku, and these studies do mention the possibilities of haiku in English. None, however, actually analyses and criticises haiku published in English. Kenneth Yasuda in *The Japanese Haiku*, for example, places the haiku form in the mainstream of literature; all his remarks point to the suitability of haiku as an English poetic form. But Yasuda (who has made, perhaps, the most comprehensive study of English-language haiku) does not explore the problems arising from the differences in background and language of the two cultures.

A monumental amount of research on Japanese literature and Oriental culture has been done by R. H. Blyth. His excellent translations of many haiku and his perceptive analyses of their cultural content have made his volumes handbooks for serious students of haiku. Two paperback volumes by Harold G. Henderson, one of translations and one entitled *Haiku in English*, have perhaps done most to popularize haiku. Translations by Peter Beilenson and more recently by Yuasa Nobuyuki have also helped to spread the knowledge of haiku, while the value of an older translator, Miyamori Asataro, must not be underestimated.

Of the volumes of English haiku published, several have originated in California. *The Way of Haiku* by James Hackett and *Borrowed Water* by the Los Altos Writers Roundtable are perhaps the best known. One "little magazine" in particular, *Haiku West*, presents a fairly high calibre of haiku in English and haiku criticism. Even more important to the student of haiku are several perceptive articles on Japanese poetry by Earl Miner, appearing in such periodicals as the *Hudson Review* and the *Bibliography of Japan Asian Studies*.

Leaning heavily on recent haiku scholarship and on ten years of experience working with the Japanese language, the writer of the present volume presents a brief explanation of the meaning and history of the haiku; a study of its cultural background centering chiefly on the search for enlightenment fundamental to Zen Buddhism; an investigation of the meaning of the haiku moment, that flash of intuition which gives birth to haiku; and, finally, three chapters dealing with haiku under the aspects of the three-line form, the seasonal elements and the poetic techniques. In general the method throughout consists in examining the Japanese form and then investigating the English form. Where possible, comparisons have been made, contrasts indicated and suggestions given. It is hoped that this book will contribute to a better understanding of haiku.

There were many people whose help made this publication possible. First of all, Mr. Jean S. Moreau of the University of Ottawa gave invaluable criticism. For an overview of the meaning of Japanese haiku, notes by Miyazaki Toshiko have been extremely helpful. English haiku used for comparison with Japanese haiku are by the following poets: Scott Alexander, Peggy Card, Helen S. Chenoweth, Molly Garling, James Hackett, Barbara Ogden Moraw, Violet Parks, Catherine Neil Paton, Anne Rutherford, Joy Shieman and Georgian Tashijian. Anita Feldman, Paul Marcotte, Frances Kirwan, Nishimura Yoshitaro, Mary O'Shaughnessy, Imaizumi Hinako and Florence Gogins added books and encouragement to perceptive suggestions. Uetani Yoshiko and Omizo Setsuko helped with translations and explanations of Japanese terms. Three librarians, Inoue Eishin, Sato Teruko and Yabuki Mihoko, traced obscure references; Patricia King, Yamano Emiko and Kohata Kiyoko did the tedious work of typing.

While this book was being written the author was on leave of absence from teaching duties at Sakura no Seibo Junior College, Fukushima, Japan. The research was financed by the Congregation de Notre Dame of

Montreal, Canada. Thanks are due to these institutions and to the persons mentioned above.

Acknowledgments are due to: Columbia University Press for excerpts from *Sources of Japanese Tradition* by Ryusaku Tsunoda, Wm. Theodore de Bary and Donald Keene (comps.); Doubleday and Company, Inc. (comps.) for excerpts from *Introduction to Haiku* by Harold G. Henderson; Grove Press, Inc. for U.S. rights for excerpts from *An Introduction to Zen Buddhism* by D. T. Suzuki; James Hackett for ten haiku from his book, *The Way of Haiku,* published by Japan Publications; Harcourt Brace Jovanovich, Inc. for excerpts from *Structural Essentials of English* by Harold Whitehall; Hokuseido Press for haiku translations and excerpts from *A History of Haiku,* Volumes I and II, *Haiku,* Volumes I to IV and *Zen in English Literature and Oriental Classics* by R. H. Blyth; The Hutchinson Publishing Group, Ltd. for British Commonwealth rights for excerpts from *An Introduction to Zen Buddhism* by D. T. Suzuki; *The Hudson Review* for selections from "The Technique of Japanese Poetry," by Earl Miner, reprinted by permission from the *Hudson Review*, Volume VIII, No. 3 (Autumn, 1955), copyright © 1955 by The Hudson Review, Inc.; Leroy Kanterman for haiku by Molly Garling and Scott Alexander in *Haiku West*, published by Leroy Kanter-

THE HAIKU FORM

I | THE MEANING
OF HAIKU

The great appeal of haiku poems seems to result mainly from two qualities: their dependence on the reader's power of awareness, bringing him closer to simple, elemental truths; and their capacity to grow in meaning as they are read and reread. Before discussing at length the background and elements of haiku, it is interesting to note briefly the origin of the form as it developed from *waka, renga* and *renku*. A short history of the growth of haiku may clarify points which follow in later chapters. An introduction to Basho, Buson, Issa and Shiki as the four undisputed masters of haiku and a description of the variation of haiku known as *senryu*, as well as an overview of developments in English haiku, are necessary preliminaries to any study of the form.

According to Miyazaki Toshiko,[1] the word "haiku" comes from *haikai renga no hokku* (the introductory lines of light linked verse). The name "haiku" was not given to the form until the late nineteenth century, when the poet Shiki, using the Japanese genius for telescoping words, invented it. A haiku is actually the first part of a *waka*, a highly conventionalized syllabic verse of five lines arranged in a sequence of 5–7–5–7–7 syllables, also known as a *tanka* or *uta*; the *tanka* and *uta* date back to the eighth-century poetry anthology, the *Manyoshu*. By the time the *Shinkokinshu* was written in the Kamakura period (1185–1333), the *waka* was beginning to decline and the *renga* was becoming popular.

Renga, or linked verse, is a sort of poetic dialogue, a succession of *waka* in which the first three lines of 5–7–5 syllables are composed by one person, the next two lines of 7–7 by another person, the following three lines of 5–7–5 by a third person, and so on; in this way, a group of four or five people sometimes composed *renga* of a hundred verses or so. Of these long composite poems, the first three lines, called *hokku*, are always the most important and the best known, much in the same way that the first verse and chorus of a popular song are often well known and the other verses ignored except by a very few.

Renga were composed at verse-capping meetings, according to rules reputedly laid down in 1186 by Fujiwara Sadaie (1162–1241) and Fujiwara Sadatake (1139?–1202). Iio Sogi (1421–1502), a poet of the Muromachi period (1392–1568) is credited with raising haiku to the level of literature by his cultivated and artistic *renga*. (Sogi is known as "the best composer under heaven.") He, as well as Yamazaki Sokan (1465–1553), Nishiyama Soin (1605–1682) and others rebelled against the conventions of the court *renga* which followed the stilted *waka* rules. They began to include words from any type of vocabulary, and to insinuate humor into their poetry. In other words, they retained the *renga* form, but discarded the *waka* spirit. This earthier type of linked verse was called *renku* but the first three lines were still called *hokku*. The new *renku* was also known as *haikai renga*, and gradually the word *haikai* by itself came to have the same meaning as *hokku*. Thus, haiku before the time of Shiki (1867–1902) were known as *hokku* or *haikai*.

The best *renga* and *waka* teachers had the habit of composing *hokku* ahead of time to have them ready when they might be needed for a linked-verse party. *Hokku* were probably among the world's shortest poems, so it was all the more necessary to try very hard to blend artistic content and form. It was Matsuo Basho (1644–1694) who succeeded in raising *haikai* from mere vers de société to the level of real literature expressing a meaningful reaction to reality beyond simple wit and humor.

Matsuo Basho was born in Iga province (Mie prefecture). As a youth he was the companion of the son of his feudal lord in Kyoto. Here he learned the tea ceremony and studied *haikai* with the poet Kitamura

Kigin (1623–1705). After the death of his young friend and patron, Basho moved to Edo (Tokyo) where he built his "banana-tree (*basho*) hermitage" in Fukugawa, and worked seriously at writing *haikai*. Wishing to taste deeply of nature and of human life he observed them carefully, finally finding his own independent voice in a subjective type of *haikai* which revealed his feelings through sound, form and image. His *haikai* are noted for their melancholy content (called *wabi*, a term from the tea ceremony applied to the aesthetic beauty of humble things) and for their quiet tone (called *sabi*, a term meaning the subdued elegance found in old, worn things).

Basho's style of *haikai* is called *shofu haikai*, from *sho*, the second syllable of his name, and *fu* (style). The belief that nature is the realm par excellence of poetry is the fundamental tenet of *shofu haikai*.

Throughout his life, Basho made many journeys in search of material for his haiku, at the same time becoming increasingly aware of nature. Of his many travel diaries, *Sarashina Kiko* (A Visit to Sarashina Village) and *Oku no Hosomichi* (The Narrow Road to the Deep North) are important, among other things, for their nature essays and haiku. He is called the Shakespeare of haiku because of his great contribution to the form. After the death of Basho, the art of *haikai* declined momentarily, but it was renewed and revivified by Buson, Issa and Shiki.

Taniguchi (or Yosano) Buson (1715–1783) was born near Osaka. Little is known of his life, but his love of painting is revealed in his picturesque, objective imagery. In his personal reserve as an artist and in his attention to his craft he might be compared to Alexander Pope, the neoclassical eighteenth-century poet, but in his penchant for experimentation he is closer to the romantics. Feeling no necessity to reveal his own emotions, he nevertheless often wrote with a warm human touch.

> *Oikaze ni*
> *Susuki karitoru*
> *Okina kana*

> An old man
> Cutting pampas grass
> The wind behind him.*

The picture of the old man bowing as the grass is bowing is clear-cut, yet sympathetically presented.

If Buson resembles the Augustans, there is no doubt that Kobayashi Issa (1763–1827) may be termed a romantic. Born in the village of Kashiwaba, north of Tokyo, he was orphaned early in life. This tragedy, however, failed to embitter him. Rather, it gave him

* Where no other translator is identified, all translations and romanizations from Japanese and Chinese in this volume are by R. H. Blyth.

a sense of kinship with small animals and insect life.
He is noted for the personal quality of his poetry, for
his spirit of rebellion against poetic and religious con-
vention and, above all, for the simple diction of his
haiku and their depiction of ordinary human affairs.

> *Koromogae*
> *Kaete mo tabi no*
> *Shirami kana*

> The change of clothes;
> Changed, yes,
> But the same lice of my journeying.

It is a familiar and disheartening experience, in an
overcrowded country, that it is difficult to get rid of
lice.

Next in time to Issa comes the modern poet Masa-
oka Shiki (1867–1902). Born in Matsuyama, Shiki
worked for a newspaper after graduating from Tokyo
University. Although he had earlier contracted tuber-
culosis, he fought in the Sino-Japanese war (1894–
1895). Returning with his illness aggravated, he
worked from his sickbed on the renewal and improve-
ment of *waka* and haiku, editing the famous haiku
magazine *Hototogisu* (*Cuckoo*). Shiki is the first poet to
use the term "haiku." He gives new characteristics to
the form—greater variety of subject matter and in-

creased objectivity. That he is an admirer of Buson's descriptive haiku may be seen by the following:

> *Iriguchi ni*
> *Mugi hosu ie ya*
> *Furu-sudare*

> Barley drying
> In front of the door:
> Old bamboo blinds hanging.

This poem presents an objective, almost harsh picture of a farmhouse.

In recent times, with the recommendation of a freer verse style by the poet Ogiwara Seisensui (b. 1884), the new tendency towards greater freedom in haiku begins. Experiments are made with titles, with two-line haiku or with longer lines. For example, the following haiku has 24 syllables divided into 10, 6 and 8 syllables to the line.

> *Hibari tenjo de naki*
> *Daichi de naki*
> *Nakinagara nobori*

> The lark sings in heaven
> Sings on earth
> Sings as it rises.

Blyth remarks that the rhythm of this verse by Seisen-sui "expresses the flight of the bird and its song."[2] Each of the four great haiku writers illustrates a certain style of haiku, and each (with the exception of Issa) left a school of followers to continue his work. One of the early developments was *senryu*.

Senryu is the satirical form of haiku originated by Karai Senryu (1718–1790) in Edo. As mock haiku, it allows greater liberty of diction including the use of vulgarisms; it also permits more obvious humour, moralizing and philosophical comment. More than haiku, perhaps indeed in opposition to haiku, it expresses the incongruity of things. The tone is less elevated than that of haiku. As Geoffrey Bownas states, "it stops short at the particular and deals in distortions and failings, not in the beauty of nature."[3]

> When she wails
> At the top of her voice,
> The husband gives in.

This *senryu* contains a universally humorous situation, indicating human failings on the part of both persons. Mothers-in-law, the clergy, shrewish wives, women of easy virtue and bachelor life are favorite targets of *senryu*. Would-be writers of English haiku are often dismayed to have their Japanese friends remark, "Your poem is more like *senryu*. It is too philosophical." It is not surprising, therefore, that *senryu* appeals strongly to Western readers. The Western tradition of logic rather than intuition makes *senryu* in some respects easier to write than haiku.

Having traced the growth of haiku from *waka* to the modern free haiku, and keeping in mind above all the *haikai* of Basho, a tentative definition of haiku may be attempted at this point. A haiku is a 17-syllable poem arranged in three lines of 5, 7 and 5 syllables, having some reference to the season and expressing the poet's union with nature.

Haiku is short; the Japanese like to call it "the first in the world for shortness." Seventeen syllables, for reasons which will be clarified later, is judged to be the number usually most suitable for haiku; similarly the three-line form is found best to support the imagery of haiku. The season word adds a whole atmosphere to the poem, thus permitting brevity without loss of significance. The raison d'être, the whole purpose of the poem, is to express the poet's union with nature, his flash of intuition concerning the objects which his senses perceive. The same definition will be seen to apply equally well to English haiku.

Once Japan was opened to the West in 1868, envoys from England became interested in translating and studying haiku. Later, Ezra Pound and the Imagists were influenced by the short poems. At present there is a growing interest in the form, as evidenced by the fact that in North America there are at least four "little magazines" devoted to the publication of haiku in English. Translations of Japanese haiku are very popular; Miyamori Asataro, R. H. Blyth, Harold G. Henderson, Peter Beilenson and Yuasa Nobuyuki are among the better-known translators. Although the translators have used a variety of forms, those who write English haiku have been, on the whole, faithful to the three-line form. Greater freedom is taken with regard to the 17 syllables.

The haiku form has been in existence in Japan for centuries and is still vigorous there. Whether or not the genuine haiku will take root and flourish in English-speaking countries remains to be seen. There is no doubt, however, that a knowledge of haiku has been found to be an enriching experience which the West seems to be welcoming with increased respect.

II | INTRODUCTION TO ZEN AND JAPANESE CULTURE

No complete discussion of haiku is possible without mentioning Zen. Yet the Zen content of haiku is little understood and often ignored by would-be writers of English haiku. Zen Buddhism has its roots in the religion founded in India by Gautama, the first form of which was Theravada or Hinayana (Lesser Vehicle) Buddhism, a later development being Mahayana (Greater Vehicle) Buddhism. When it entered China, the Indian religion assimilated elements of Taoism and Confucianism and found practical expression in Ch'an (Zen) Buddhism. Chinese painting and poetry were permeated with these religious influences. Eventually, the several branches of Buddhism, along with Chinese literature and art, were introduced into Japan, where they came into contact with Shinto, the indigenous religion of the country. The search for the *satori* of Zen was associated with several typically Japanese forms of art—Noh, the tea ceremony, flower arranging and the code of chivalry.

These religious and artistic influences all culminate in the Zen *satori*, or moment of enlightenment, the concept of which will be examined briefly later.

BUDDHISM, TAOISM AND CONFUCIANISM

Zen is a development of the Buddhism founded in India by Gautama Buddha in the sixth century B.C. In his first sermon, Gautama taught that there are two extremes to be avoided—sensual indulgence and self-mortification. By avoiding the two extremes he gained the enlightenment of the middle path. The Four Noble Truths of the middle path are, first, the Truth of Pain or Suffering—the pains of birth, old age, sickness, death, union with the unpleasant, separation from the pleasant and the pain of not obtaining what one wishes; secondly, the Truth of the Cause of Pain, which is craving—lustfulness, the craving for existence and the craving for nonexistence; thirdly, the truth of the Cessation of Pain: that is, the cessation of craving and detachment from it; and lastly, the Truth of the Path that Leads to the Cessation of Pain—the eightfold path, the final goal of which is Nirvana. Nirvana is a transcendent state free of craving, suffering and sorrow, the state of freedom from the self and absorption into the great Self, analogous to that of a candle held against the sun; the candle retains its identity yet merges with the light of the sun. The essence of the doctrine of Gautama may be summed up as transience and detachment—the transience of life and the detachment from its joys and sorrows which is necessary for the faithful. These two religious notions are prevalent in haiku.

As Buddhism developed, the earlier version came to be known as Hinayana or Theravada (Lesser Vehicle) Buddhism, a later version as Mahayana (Greater Vehicle). The essential difference between the two is that, whereas the goal of Hinayana Buddhism is Nirvana, Mahayana Buddhism teaches that men who attain Buddhahood should turn in compassion towards their fellow men, who are all capable of being saved. The Buddhist saints who help men to attain salvation are known as bodhisattvas. According to W. E. Soothill's abridged version of *The Lotus of the Wonderful Law*, "through the inspiration and compassionate care of these bodhisattvas, all men may ultimately achieve salvation."[1] As Soothill's summary indicates, those who held the earlier teaching of Gautama did not necessarily receive the new doctrine with enthusiasm:

> [Buddha] is aware that many who have followed his earlier teachings, including the practice of severe disciplines, will feel cheated rather than be rejoiced . . . that Buddhahood is open to all . . . rather than only to the few who have prepared

themselves for the attainment of Nirvana. These are identified as followers of the Hinayana.[2]

Mahayana Buddhism was further developed by the Chinese and Japanese who adapted it to the culture of their countries. The Chinese fused it with Taoism and Confucianism and, incorporating the special Indian type of meditation called Dhyana, developed a new form of Buddhism, known as Ch'an (Zen). The Japanese welcomed all of these branches of Chinese religion and fused them with Shinto to produce new Buddhist forms, including Zen. All of these strains, but especially Zen, provided a rich cultural background for haiku.

Taoism, based on the writings of Lao-tsu (in Japanese, Roshi), dating from the sixth century B.C., received further development from Chuang-tzu (Soshi; 364?–286? B.C.). The word *Tao* (literally, "the Way") also refers to the principle of all things, antedating all things and forming their substance. It is spiritual (and therefore invisible), inaudible, vague and elusive; yet there is in it form and essence. It is nonbeing in the sense that it is prior to and above all things, and in its operation it is characterized by *wu-wei* (no action), by which is meant no unnatural action. (This may be analogous to the Greek notion of primeval stasis.) Natural action, which leads to a life of peace, harmony and enlightenment, is compared to weak, yielding things—water, woman, an infant. There is nothing better than water for attacking strong, hard things. The great stress on natural simplicity and on a life of plainness—in which profit is discarded, cleverness abandoned, selfishness eliminated and desires reduced —is essentially a romantic emphasis. Lao-tsu also emphasized the phenomenon of change. Yet all things are one, for Tao embraces them and combines them, uniting transcendental mysticism with dynamic realism. The outstanding characteristic of popular Taoism is its simple desire for heaven, according to an early Japanese Buddhist, Kukai, who wrote of the ten stages of religious experience.

> The mind infantile and without fears.
> The pagan hopes for birth in heaven, there for a
>   while to know peace.
> He is like an infant, like a calf that follows its
>   mother.[3]

In the interaction of the two religions, Taoists assimilated Buddhist ideas while Buddhism took over Taoist philosophic terms as well as the concepts of being and nonbeing. Taoism's greatest influence on Buddhism was in the development of Zen Buddhism. As an example of Taoist influence on haiku, there is a poem by Basho which is almost proverbial among educated Japanese:

Mono ieba
Kuchibiru samushi
Aki no kaze

When I speak,
My lips feel cold—
The autumn wind.

This resembles closely the verse of Lao-tsu:

Those who know, speak not.
Those who speak, know not.

Miyamori Asataro writes of Basho's haiku that it is a didactic verse which means: "Keep silence, otherwise evil will overtake you."[4]

The thought of Confucius, also fused with Buddhism, was subsequently to influence Zen. Confucianism, while inculcating strong attachment to duty, emphasized the happiness flowing from obedience to the various commitments of husbands and wives, parents and children, brothers and sisters, men and their friends, rulers and their subjects. Thus society was a great, utopian family, in which all enjoyed the rights of age and status. It was upheld by spiritual forces, especially the complex of "Love Powers" which are continually radiating from human hearts. Confucianism in Japan, in its stress on loyalty to one's superior, helped to foster the austere, Zen-loving warrior class to which Basho belonged. To haiku this religion contributed, according to R. H. Blyth, "a certain sobriety, reserve . . . brevity and pithiness, and a moral flavour that may sometimes be vaguely felt, but is never allowed to be separated . . . from the poetry itself."[5] The rationalism of Confucius is a "classical" influence in contrast to the "romantic" influence of Taoism.

INFLUENCE OF CHINESE POETRY AND ART

Even greater than the influence of Confucianism was the effect on haiku of the Chinese poetry which entered Japan with Buddhism. This poetry, for all its romance, nostalgia, world-weariness (and also, at least according to Ezra Pound, its pure colour) is, above all, permeated with Ch'an Buddhism and Taoism. A comparison of Chinese and Japanese poetry reveals that Chinese poetry deals with vast vistas, whereas Japanese poetry tends to focus attention on the small; where Chinese poetry presents the historical past, Japanese poetry presents the individual past in an historical setting. Chinese poetry will describe space in terms of ranges of mountains, whereas Japanese poetry will describe it in the sky of day and night. Two types of Chinese poems in particular appeal to the Japanese—those speaking of a life of solitude, showing the Ch'an Buddhist influence, and those describing rain. (There are

scores of synonyms for rain in the Japanese language.)
Because the Chinese poet is in tune with the Taoist
universe, his poetry reflects the world as in an undis-
torted mirror. What he expresses as personal feeling is
also universal law. His poetry is suprapersonal, extra-
personal. He stands outside his own personal attitudes
and regards them objectively, as do Basho and Buson,
who are both particularly influenced by Chinese po-
etry. Basho absorbs the Chinese influence completely
and then produces his own new and different poetry
with almost no borrowing, as can be seen by compar-
ing Basho's haiku with Lao-tsu's saying (see p. 30).
Buson takes whole phrases from Chinese poets but
puts them into new settings and gives them new
meaning.

> *Shosho no*
> *Kari no namida ya*
> *Oboro-zuki*

> Tears
> For the wild geese of Shosho;
> A hazy moon.

This poem was written by Buson, as he states, while
listening to the lute one evening. It echoes verses by
the famous Chinese poet Senki:

—Returning Wild Geese—

Why do they so blindly depart from Shosho?
The water is blue, the sand is white, the moss on
  both banks green;
Should the lute of twenty-five strings be played,
  on a moonlit night,
With the overwhelming emotion will they not
  return?

Blyth states that the lute of 25 strings was played by
Gao and Joei, the two daughters of Gyo, who both
died at this spot. The "tears" of Buson's verse are con-
nected with the two sisters.[6]

Chinese art, as well as Chinese poetry, reflects reli-
gion and influences haiku deeply. The romantic Chi-
nese paintings are Taoistic in that they show men as
very small beings amid overpoweringly intense land-
scapes. By comparison the *sumi-e* (black-and-white ink
drawings) introduced into Japan by Zen priests are ex-
tremely simple. These intuitive drawings express the
essence of the subject in a few rough, uncorrected
brush strokes. This essence is more important than
technique or beauty. From *sumi-e* developed *haiga*,
small pictures in black and white or in simple colours
on the same paper as a haiku. They either illustrate the
haiku,, saying the same thing in a different way, or
they reinforce it by introducing a new concept, thus

deepening the meaning of the haiku. It was Zen which appropriated both Chinese art and Chinese poetry and placed them at the disposal of haiku.

SHINTO

Having gathered richness and depth in China, Mahayana Buddhism was to encounter further enriching and deepening influences: the indigenous Japanese religion, Shinto, and the Japanese genius for absorbing alien cultural strains and adding its own characteristics to them. The word Shinto means "the way of the gods." Maurius B. Jansen, Professor of History at Princeton University, describing Shinto, writes that

> the spontaneous response to nature and beauty found an early and enduring focus in the cult of Shinto, with whose gods the Japanese first peopled their island home. Conceived as a relatively simple expression of awe and gratitude before the forces of nature, Shinto ritual invoked the spirits helpful to agricultural pursuits. The Sun Goddess was the highest of a myriad of deities who had brought forth the divine land of Japan. Since she was the progenitress of the Imperial clan, her cult associated religion with government and provided an important point of continuity throughout Japanese history. Shinto taught little of morality

or worship, and its gods were approached by ceremonial purification and ablution.

The purification festivals are popular to this day. Recent student demonstrations by young men and women may be said to be an echo of those religious processions (in which, however, young men only took part). Jansen sees the Shinto cult as essentially

> the work of an agricultural people who saw in natural settings and phenomena the condition of their survival. The association of religion with cleanliness, the seasonal communal festivals, the expression of communal joy and gratitude . . . all were aspects of the joyous and uncomplicated reponse to nature . . . made through Shinto.[7]

The communal aspect of Shinto did dovetail nicely with the utopian theories of Confucianism. But the Shinto word *kami* (translated into English by "gods") really indicates the animism which is the essence of Shinto. Animism is a primitive belief which endows even inanimate things with both life and spirit to explain two phenomena: first, the difference between a living man and a corpse (described as caused by the disappearance of life from the body), and secondly, the existence of dreams (explained as the ability of the spirit to move about.) Shinto, with its belief in the many *kami* or minor deities of mountains, streams and trees, is a religion of nature worship. This fact is reflected in the large part played by nature in Japanese haiku.

ZEN AND ZEN ARTS

Although Buddhism as it arrived in Japan included six sects, the Zen sect, emphasizing the practical application of doctrine, had the greatest influence on haiku.

The word *Zen* means "meditation." The central and most strongly stressed teaching was that through meditation one could attain *satori* (enlightenment), intuitive insight into what transcends logical distinctions. An aid to the attainment of *satori* was meditation on *koan* paradoxes like, "Thinking not of good, thinking not of evil, what is your own original face, which you had before you were born?"[8] Only by ridding the mind of conscious logical distinctions and by reaching into the unconscious could one solve the *koan*. The intuition of Zen was not to be found by research into books. Indeed, books were frowned upon as distractions. Although the *koan* explanations and poems were written by Zen masters, there is a famous incident of a monk burning books because his disciples were becoming preoccupied with them. He claimed that instead of looking at the moon they were looking at the finger which was pointing to the moon. It cannot be overemphasized that false intuition, contrived insight and mere cleverness were abhorred in the practice of Zen and in the arts, as will be seen later. An analogy exists in the concept that while piety and love are great virtues, false piety and false love are great vices.

Illustrations of the spirit of Zen may be shown by three anecdotes.

The Zen master Hakuin was praised by his neighbors as one living a pure life.

A beautiful Japanese girl whose parents owned a good store lived near him. Suddenly, without any warning, her parents discovered she was with child.

This made her parents angry. She would not confess who the man was, but after much harrassment at last named Hakuin.

In great anger the parents went to the master. "Is that so?" was all he would say.

After the child was born it was brought to Hakuin. By this time he had lost his reputation, which did not trouble him, but he took very good care of the child. He obtained milk from his neighbors and everything else the little one needed. A year later the girl-mother could stand it no longer. She told her parents the truth—that the real father of the child was a young man who worked in the fishmarket.

The mother and father of the girl at once went to Hakuin to ask his forgiveness, to apologize at length, and to get the child back again.

Hakuin was willing. In yielding the child, all he would say was: "Is that so?"[9]

Hakuin was detached from his reputation. He had an enlightened view of the true value of things in this life. Like the resurrected Lazarus in Browning's poem "The Epistle," he was undisturbed by events which would upset an unenlightened man. For Hakuin, contradictions and disturbances were harmonized in a unity of a higher order.

A second anecdote concerns the master Sosan. His disciple Doshin asked him how to become free. Sosan in turn asked Doshin who bound him. The disciple had to admit sheepishly that no one bound him. "Why then do you seek freedom?" said the master.[10]

This anecdote illustrates the Zen adept's avoidance of dialectic. Sosan went right to the heart of the problem. Who bound him? The disciple wanted to philosophize. He was seeking an excuse for his faults in his imagined lack of liberty. He was devious and unenlightened. The master of Zen, on the other hand, condemns convoluted thinking. For him, ordinary, everyday life and behaviour are the real way of Zen.

Lastly, a monk asked Joshu, "Has a dog Buddha-nature or not?" The monk answered: "Mu." The answer *mu* or *wu* is the prefix "non" or "no," but it also imitates the "woof" that a dog might answer if asked the question. This *mu* or nothingness is the road to enlightenment.

While meditating on *koan* such as the anecdote of Joshu's dog, the monks used haiku, *haiga* (haiku pictures) and other arts as disciplines to foster enlightenment and awareness of essences; according to Asano Nagatake, Director of Tokyo's National Museum, "a new kind of artistic endeavor was born as disciples tried to express spiritual concepts in objective form."[11]

Earle Ernst explains the nature of existence as taught in Japanese Buddhism:

> Existence consists in the interplay of a plurality of elements whose true nature is indescribable and whose source is unknown. Combinations of these elements instantaneously flash into existence and instantaneously disappear, to be succeeded by new combinations of elements appearing in a strict causality. . . . The only concrete reality is the moment, which like the image from a single frame of motion picture film is . . . followed by a new and different frame and image. The visible world is therefore flamelike, shifting and evanescent, possessed of no durable validity.[12]

It must be stressed that the Japanese artist, too, regards

the world of perception as having no permanence, only brief flashes of actuality. He merely records; he does not interpret. He concentrates on single moments of time and space.

Bushido (the way of the warrior), based on Zen and Confucian principles, stresses frugality of life, benevolence and righteousness. *Bushi* means "samurai, warrior"; *do* means "way." *Bushido* is "the way of the samurai" or simply "chivalry." Loyalty to the warrior's lord is more important even than loyalty to the laws of the country or to the duties towards the family. If a conflict arose between the two, the duty to the lord should be performed, followed by *seppuku* (suicide by disembowelment) to atone for the offense against the law or against family ties. In modern Japan lifelong loyalty and service to one's employer go far beyond anything found in Western countries. Thus Basho, a young man from a samurai family, first became interested in haiku out of loyalty to his young lord, a *haikai*-lover who died at an early age. The Zen frugality and simplicity of living arrangements; the mingled sense of pride and tragedy flowing from the spirit of sacrifice epitomized by samurai suicides; these are the chief contributions of *bushido* to haiku.

The Zen Buddhist concept of life as a succession of moments, whose meaning is to be captured by openness to the significance of each event as it occurs, gave birth to many new arts. One of these is *cha no yu* (the tea ceremony). According to Asano, its purpose was "to look quietly into oneself and to appreciate nature while meditating within a rustic teahouse."[13] Each part of the teahouse is a work of art having a certain symbolism. The overhang of the roof above the entrance indicates the changeability of the weather and of human life. The opening is small (three feet square), so that the guest must humble himself by stooping. Outside the house the stepping-stones, the water basin and the stone lantern indicate a willingness to be used: the stones to be trodden upon; the water to remove the dirt of the hands and mouth in the ceremonial purification; the wick of the lantern to be consumed. The teahouse itself is small and simple (nine feet square or smaller) suggesting refined poverty by the simple materials chosen carefully. The founders of the tea ceremony emphasized harmony and respect among the guests and utensils, cleanliness and the tranquillity flowing from the unhurried handling of aesthetically beautiful articles mellowed by long and loving use. If enlightenment is not attained within the teahouse, at least the guest is reminded of the proper spirit in which to meditate and his whole being is opened to the workings of events.

Ikebana, flower-arranging, demands a steady concentration on nature, a union with it, and a reduction of its complexity by a limiting of its profusion of material to the point where its true nature is shown. The components of a classical flower arrangement represent seven elements—the mountain peak, a waterfall, a hill, the foot of the mountain, the town and the division of the whole into *in* (shade) and *yo* (sun). *In* and *yo* also represent *yin* and *yang*, passive and active, the female and male principles of Taoist philosophy. The three branches in some arrangements are called *shin* (truth), *soe* (supporting) and *nagashi* (flowing). Their asymmetric form suggests the universe. The principle of compression of nature as found in *ikebana* is an aid to Zen enlightenment. It is similar to the compression of haiku, which records an image of nature at a significant moment.

The discipline of concentration and economy of means which characterizes *ikebana* is also found in Noh, where the isolation of a significant moment is the visual climax in a performance. Stillness represents a perfect balance of opposed forces. Stillness also represents movement; for example, the actor, in slowly raising one still hand to within a few inches of the eyes, represents passionate weeping. There is a strange contradiction between the reality of the feelings and the conventionality of the acting. The dream world is yet the real world.[14] Noh represents a series of important single moments in the wheel of life, in contrast to the Western emphasis on flow shown in the actor's face.

In all these varied activities, *satori* is the element constantly sought. In the examination of Zen arts, four things have been noted—contemplation of nature, meditation on *koan*, *bushido* and artistic expression—in poetry, visual art, the theatre, flower arranging and the tea ceremony. In all these the constant element was the search for, or expression of, *satori*, the end and aim of Zen life. *Satori* gives man a new viewpoint, a new way of seeing the ordinary things of life.

Daisetz Teitaro Suzuki, the great Zen scholar, has pointed out that two men can look at the same thing, one without the viewpoint of Zen, and one with this viewpoint:

> The object of Zen discipline consists in acquiring a new viewpoint for looking into the essence of things. . . . You and I are supposedly living in the same world, but who can tell that the thing we popularly call a stone that is lying before my window is the same to both of us? You and I sip a cup of tea. That act is apparently alike to us both, but who can tell what a wide gap there is subjectively between your drinking and my drinking? In your drinking there may be no Zen, while mine is brim-full of it. The reason for it is: you move in a logical circle and I am out of it.[15]

The man without *satori* is too logical. *Satori* is "intuitive looking-into, in contra-distinction to intellectual and logical understanding; it is the unfolding of a new world hitherto unperceived."[16] *Satori* cannot be taught; it must be sought without strain and found by each individual himself. A master, scorning books, can help a disciple orally, in a person-to-person contact, but actual *satori* can be reached and experienced by the individual only. When the conditions necessary for *satori* are in the mind ready to mature, a simple thing like the sound of a pebble hitting a tree, a stumble, the fragrance of a flower, the flash of colour in a bird will bring about enlightenment. Reality itself is perceived, Self is attained and the ordinary world is seen more clearly. Because *satori* makes life more enjoyable and meaningful, because it broadens man's horizon to include the whole universe, it is, in the opinion of the Zen Buddhist, well worth striving for.

To summarize, Zen Buddhism has grown from a centuries-old tradition of Mahayana Buddhism, Taoism and Confucianism. Many Japanese arts have thrived under and by its influence. Behind the deceptively simple haiku lies the long history of an important line of Eastern thought. Zen illuminates the thought of Basho, Buson, Issa, Shiki and others and provides the essential key to the meaning of many haiku. Since the Zen content of haiku is often little understood by English would-be writers of haiku, aspects of Zen found in Japanese and English haiku will be examined in more detail in the next chapter.

III

THE HAIKU MOMENT

The *satori* of Zen is analogous to what Kenneth Yasuda calls the haiku moment. Just as *satori* is the heart of Zen, its whole object, so the haiku moment is the heart of haiku and its source. In an effort to better understand the haiku moment, the conditions for *satori* and for the haiku moment must be examined. Each of these conditions integrates complementary and antithetical qualities; directness is linked with paradox, austerity with joy, love of nature with love of the ordinary. The avoidance of comment and clutter is common to all these qualities. As each quality is examined and illustrated in the Japanese translations, an attempt will be made to see whether haiku in English can be examined in the same way. Finally, the question of Western man's ability adequately to understand Zen concepts will be briefly considered.

The haiku moment may be defined as an instant in which man becomes united to an object, virtually becomes the object and realizes the eternal, universal truth contained in being. Yasuda describes it from the poet's point of view:

> I know that when one happens to see a beautiful sunset or lovely flowers, for instance, he is often so delighted that he merely stands still. This state of mind might be called "ah-ness" for the beholder can only give one breath-long exclamation of delight: "Ah!" The object has seized him and he is aware only of the shapes, the colors, the shadows, the blendings. In a brief moment he sees a pattern, a significance he had not seen before.[1]

The moment of "ah-ness," the haiku moment, is timeless; man is united to his environment and realizes that he partakes of the eternity of the universe. "The nature of the haiku moment is anti-temporal and its quality is eternal, for in this state man and his environment are one unified whole."[2] Basho writes of the evolution of the haiku moment:

> Go to the pine if you want to learn about the pine, or to the bamboo if you want to learn about the bamboo. And in doing so, you must leave your subjective preoccupation with yourself. Otherwise you impose yourself on the object and do not learn. Your poetry issues of its own accord when you and the object have become one—when

you have plunged deep enough into the object to see something like a hidden glimmering there. However well phrased your poetry may be, if your feeling is not natural—if the object and yourself are separate—then your poetry is not true poetry but merely your subjective counterfeit.[3]

[YUASA NOBUYUKI]

Haiku is the expression in words of the instant of intuition uniting poet and object. Basho intimates, and Yasuda agrees,[4] that the very words of the haiku are found during the instant of the haiku moment. Nevertheless, a certain amount of polishing is done afterwards. The moment makes a lasting impression which, if rendered successfully, imparts freshness and sincerity to the poem.

Sometimes a phrase that the poet uses comes from Chinese poetry, but, as the setting is completely different, the words take on a new meaning. The poet's problem is to convey (as R. H. Blyth has described it) "the power of seeing"[5] what he has seen. He wishes to share his haiku moment. This cannot be done through explanations or by cluttered sentimental verse. It is absolutely necessary for him to avoid intellection or philosophical comment, and this will be stressed repeatedly.

Haiku is sometimes called a way of life rather than an art form. Yet haiku is produced much as any other art form is produced, except perhaps that the poet expresses the reality to which he has had a significant reaction exactly as it is, with a greater avoidance of personal accretion. A poet working in another form and tradition may use images different from those immediately associated with the experience which evoked the poetic intuition. Two examples may illustrate this. "The Waste Land" by T. S. Eliot contains numerous images—of buildings and parts of buildings (stairs, ceilings), of people and parts of people (feet, hands), of rocks, of water, of hyacinths—all of which are symbolic. Eliot introduces exotic words and obscure allusions which even his own notes do not suffice to elucidate. He makes use of strange rhythms and irregular forms; yet, difficult as it is, the poem adequately expresses Eliot's intuition which, stated baldly, is that the twentieth century is unproductive and that man is groping in misery to find some meaning to life. On the other hand, the poet Basho wrote the following haiku:

> *Furu ike ya*
> *Kawazu tobikomu*
> *Mizu no oto*

> An old pond
> A frog jumps in
> The sound of the water.

Basho is expressing a moment of actual encounter. Although he did not even see the frog, when he heard the sound as it jumped into the still pond a sort of universal echo reverberated for him. The whole meaning of existence centred there. The instant of noise accented the eternal silence. T. S. Eliot expressed a significant reaction to reality (something perhaps made him realize the emptiness of modern life) by writing a symbolic poem. Basho expressed a significant reaction to reality by expressing the haiku moment, in which he became one with what he heard and intuitively realized its meaning. For the moment time stopped and he had a flash of understanding—a significant reaction to reality, but one which could be pinpointed and which at the same time brought with it a wealth of association.

The word "pinpointed" is the key to the explanation of the difference between haiku and other forms of poetry. Eliot's significant reaction to reality may be one which took place cumulatively, over a period of growing realization. Or perhaps some one event in his life provided a clash with reality which resulted in the poetic intuition. No matter how the significant reaction occurred, other objective correlatives do express his poetic knowledge in "The Waste Land." No particular object or event, therefore, can be pinpointed as the source of his intuition. In haiku, however, the source can be, indeed must be, pinpointed. Both poets reflect the philosophy of their culture. Eliot gives a complete synthesis, from many points of view, of a whole culture. Basho presents a clear, strong, simple and instant analysis of a moment of time from one point of view. The intuitive denudation reflects his philosophy that reality is an illusion. Only the present moment exists as one of an infinite number of points on a wheel. Both poets call on the reader to work. Eliot demands of the mind that order be reduced from the total work to one. Basho demands that, by meditation, from one event the total truth be found. The meaning of haiku grows. It has the power of resonation.

DIRECTNESS AND PARADOX

The meaning of the haiku moment may be clarified by an examination of the qualities of mind and the related literary qualities which work to produce Zen *satori* and to express the haiku moment. The first quality is directness. The directness of Zen and haiku may be defined as the straight looking at things and portrayal of them without symbol and without metaphor. As Blyth has pointed out, when Basho looks at an onion he calls it an onion; when he feels an indistinct unnameable emotion he says so.[6] He does not tolerate vague language. When he hears the sound of a frog jumping, he calls it exactly that. His presentation of the experience illustrates directness. In the frog poem quoted already, since Basho allows the reality of the things in nature to speak for themselves, no comment is necessary about the pond other than the fact that it is old. In Japanese *furu* as used in this poem is an incomplete form of the adjective *furui*; that is, it is in the prefix form of the word and should be closely attached to a noun. In romanized letters "old pond" might more accurately be written as one word, *furuike* (old-pond), a bare, direct image. All the other words —three nouns and a verb—are pure statement.

Directness in haiku is antipathetic to symbol and metaphor. There is a great temptation for the Western reader to interpret haiku symbolically. But the things of nature are not symbols of something else. They have meaning in themselves. The pond does not symbolize eternity; the sound of the water does not symbolize an instant of time. The pond is a pond; the sound opens the mind to an intuition about eternity and time, but it is, nevertheless, simply a sound of water. They may become symbols in their resonance but only mediately, not immediately. Similarly, simile and metaphor are frowned upon in haiku as being efforts at cleverness. Directness, it cannot be repeated often enough, tends to prohibit cleverness and false intuition.

The quality of directness is not impossible in English. Modern British and American poets, influenced by Ezra Pound and the Imagists, who in turn were influenced by French Impressionism, by James McNeil Whistler's paintings, by *ukiyo-e* (genre) prints and, most significantly, by Japanese haiku—are writing compact, stripped-down, direct poetry.[7] An example of this may be found in "Thirteen Ways of Looking at a Blackbird" by Wallace Stevens. The poet speaks of an afternoon which is like a long evening, an afternoon of snow and the expectation of more snow, and of a blackbird sitting in cedar-limbs. This section, Otake Masaru claims,[8] resembles haiku more than it resembles the usual type of English poetry. He compares it to a haiku by Naito Joso (1662–1704):

> *Taka no me no*
> *Kare no ni suwaru*
> *Arashi kana*

> The eyes of the hawk
> Are looking at the dry fields
> And the coming storm.

This haiku and the stanza by Stevens share the same ominous tone of expectancy. Both birds are waiting for a storm; both are set in a winter landscape. Neither poem uses an unnecessary word; both illustrate the quality of directness. Examples could be multiplied from the work of Stevens. Some of J. W. Hackett's haiku[9] have the same quality of directness:

Deep within the stream
the huge fish lie motionless,
facing the current.

This is pared-down poetry, stating facts without symbolism or comment. No false intuition, no mere cleverness can be found. On the other hand, although Ezra Pound was aiming at directness in his famous Metro poem, the work fails as haiku. The poet's metaphor comparing the faces in the crowd to petals on a black bough does not make the relationship clear enough. Both John Gould Fletcher and Kenneth Yasuda agree on this point. Yasuda explains that "the poem is lacking in unity, in that forceful intensity of poetic vision and insight which alone can weld the objects named into a meaningful whole."[10]

It is probably true to say that the complement of directness is paradoxicality. A paradox is a statement seemingly absurd, yet in fact true. It results from the inability of words to express two things at once; for example, it is really impossible for words to express the fact that a man can possess nothing and everything at the same time, as a poem by Yamaguchi Sodo (1643–1716) states:

Yado no haru
Nani mo naki koso
Nani mo are

> In my hut this spring
> There is nothing.
> There is everything.

Materially there is nothing. In the man's spiritual contentment there is everything. Zen and haiku abound in such fascinating paradoxes, which have been attempted also in English haiku, such as this one by James Hackett:

> Half of the minnows
> within this sunlit shallow
> are not really there.

Half of the minnows that are there are not there; this is an apparent contradiction. Upon reflection, it is understood that many fish can be seen, but half of them are shadows.

The danger of conscious striving for paradox, intellection and explicit judgment in writing English haiku cannot be overemphasized. To the Japanese mind, the following poem by Hackett might seem to contain too much explicit judgment, in the form of philosophical comment:

> That old empty house,
> now so overgrown with years,
> is the only real one here.

AUSTERITY AND JOY

Austerity is another Zen quality which militates against comment and overintellection. The austerity recommended by Zen may be defined as a poverty which, while allowing the bare necessities of life, eschews superfluities for the sake of the detachment, silence, simplicity and loneliness which come with privation. For a haiku poet the expression of austerity is twofold: first, in his life of detachment, and second, in his sparing use of words. Basho is the model par excellence on both counts; he desired actually to feel want in order to come closer to nature—a desire which prompted him to undertake his long and difficult journeys—and in his haiku his austerity is reflected in their complete lack of conceit and ornamentation. Among poets in English, Wallace Stevens understood the austerity of haiku. Equally at home in the heat of Florida and the cold of New England, Stevens depicts nature in both these settings with the true haiku touch. In addition to the humour of the haiku master, he shows the austerity of philosophers like Basho and other writers who are close to the Japanese haiku tradition. Stevens was familiar with and appreciative of Asian art. He has drawn his own spiritual biography in "The Comedian as the Letter C," where the destitute Crispin is a true son of Basho. The American who sings of fleas and insects is close to Basho and Issa, and to the many haiku poets who did the same. Also, Crispin learns from everyday, ordinary things like signboards and window panes, a trait which is characteristic of haiku writers. He is aware of his own growth and his progress from the observation of things to the understanding of "concrete universals." Crispin's austerity is found not only in his way of life but in his disciplined art. Considering Stevens's work, it seems that poets writing in English can understand and adequately express the haiku spirit of austerity.

The haiku poet is austere for the sake of detachment. As illustrated in the story of Hakuin, he is able to hold himself aloof and to regard events and things, even those which concern himself, in an objective way. He does not see things as he would like to see them, but as they are. Buson gives us a picture of a peony:

> *Botan chitte*
> *Uchikasanarinu*
> *Nisanpen*

> The peony has fallen
> A few scattered petals
> Lie one on another.

This is typical Buson picture-painting. The Japanese version is more austere than the English—the peony falling, the piled-up petals, two or three. Objectivity in writing of nature is found in the Buson-like poem by Hackett already quoted:

> Deep within the stream
> the huge fish lie motionless,
> facing the current.

Here is English haiku at its best. The poet simply states the fact without making any philosophical comments upon it, simply states the fact without making any comparisons, judgments or conclusions. In a word, he is detached.

Yet, in stating that the Zen disciple is detached, it is not implied that he indulges in self-hate. On the contrary, while being detached from self, while being unselfish, he is more aware than most men of the self's importance. As Blyth says, in a seeming paradox, "though this self is so important, it is only by the obliteration of self that anything can be known, that anything can be truly done."[11] Self must not get in the way of perception. Zen causes men to live intensely, to do everything as well as they can, whatever their activity may be, and whatever the consequences. As Blyth says, "Zen takes a man as he is, and raises him to his highest power."[12] Basho says the same thing when he describes the cicada singing his best even though he is to die very soon.

Yagate shinu
Keshiki wa miezu
Semi no koe

Nothing intimates,
In the voice of the cicada,
How soon it will die.

If all is evanescent, a moment is equal to a century. This is the strength and the weakness of haiku—the strength, because of the great insight which can be gained in a moment, the weakness, because in the effort to portray evanescence, haiku is sometimes pared down to nothing, failing to encompass the organic nature of experience. In the case of Hackett's huge fish—they are, like the cicada, being true to their nature, perfect Zen fish, lying motionless in deep water with their noses pointed exactly the right way.

The austerity of Zen calls for a simplicity which may be defined as a lack of complication. Simplicity may be twofold—first, with regard to the objects contemplated, and second, with regard to the manner in which the contemplation occurs. Haiku has both kinds of simplicity, as is illustrated by Basho, who found happiness even in trivial things:

Iza kodomo
Hashiriarukan
Tama-arare

Look, children
Hail-stones!
Let's rush out!

This shows that Basho was the type of man described by Mencius, "the great man is he who does not lose his childlike heart," and Lao-tsu, "he is like a child alone, careless, unattached, devoid of ambition."[13] Among English poets, William Blake and Emily Dickinson have this childlike quality to a high degree. This is illustrated in such haiku-like poems as "The Fly" by Blake and "The Road Was Lit with Moon and Star" by Dickinson. Joyous simplicity in observing humble creatures is also shown by Hackett:

This garter snake
goes in and out of the grass
all at the same time!

The childlike wonder at the discovery of the characteristic ability of the snake to go in and out simultaneously is good Zen. The simplicity of the language, especially "goes in and out" and "at the same time" is in keeping with the simplicity of the thought. Once again, as has been seen in the study of other qualities, the absence of comment contributes to the power of the haiku.

The complement to Zen austerity is joy, or the lively gusto which goes hand in hand with austerity and flows from it. The union of joy and austerity is earthy rather than ethereal. It combines a grateful acceptance of and sympathy for all creatures with a saving sense of humour which prevents the poet from taking himself too seriously and which allows him to achieve the balanced insight necessary to produce real haiku. This joy produces a lightheartedness like that of Saint Francis of Assisi, which led him to dance and sing before the Lord as he took delight in all living creatures. As in the tradition of Hasidic Judaism,[14] the joyous man feels that whatever happens is inevitable. Happiness or sadness, our own shortcomings or those of others— all are accepted with a joy which causes the poet never to refuse to give anything and never to refuse to receive anything. To put it more positively, he is always open, generous and thankful in the face of all creatures and all events. This grateful joy is manifest in a poem by Issa.

> *Ogi nite*
> *Shaku wo toraseru*
> *Botan kana*

> The peony
> Made me measure it
> With my fan.

Issa is so united to nature, so open to other things, such

as the peony, that they can command him without fear. A Westerner may also be open to the desires of things:

> Sometimes the oddest thing,
> like this orange pip,
> begs not to be thrown away.

It is not stated, however, that the poet slipped it into his pocket. The compulsion is not so great in Hackett's poem as in Issa's. Overflowing joy is expressed in the following verse by the same American author:

> Reading this sutra,
> I suddenly began to laugh . . .
> without knowing why.

This is the foolishness of the "holy fool" kind (not to be confused with silliness) which is part of the joy of giving up a possessive attitude towards things. Reading the scriptures can fill the heart with such joy that it erupts in pure animal high spirits. The sutra reader who laughs does not stop to analyse why; he merely accepts the exhilarated feeling without trying to explain it. Joy and gusto lead the poet to enjoy a joke at his own expense and not be afraid to expose his own weakness. Again this agrees with Hasidic tradition.[15] The haiku poet Watanabe Suiha (1872–1946) wrote:

Jakumaku to
Tampo ni ashi wo
Soroe keri

In the solitude
I put my feet together
Upon the hot-water bottle.

The word *tampo*, which is colloquial for *yutampo* (hot-water bottle), fits in with the humour of the poem. The word *soroe* means to line up something neatly, often used to indicate the putting together of the hands and feet for a polite bow. This connotation enhances the humour. The gusto of haiku is akin to that of Shakespeare's song, from *Love's Labour's Lost*, "When Icicles Hang by the Wall," especially the last line, "While greasy Joan doth keel [cool] the pot." Real poetry can use any material. The important thing is that it be judiciously, infallibly, inevitably selected and arranged so that the perfect form is found, and so that the poet expresses the truth as it is. Otherwise the exuberant haiku penetrates too far across the fringe of *senryu*, where social comment is implied. At the risk of redundancy, let it be repeated: in the expression of lively joy there is statement, but without comment.

LOVE OF NATURE AND THE ORDINARY

The Zen attitude towards nature is seminal to an

understanding of haiku. As is evident from the examples given thus far, the Japanese love of nature is intense and without sentimentality. Two currents—Zen and Shinto—imply a kinship among all creatures because of an intuition of shared reality. Every single creature acts according to its nature, doing what it was made to do. This rule extends even to inanimate objects, such as the humble rocks with only the top third showing, in a Zen monk's garden—a garden which captures the essence of nature's woods, waterfalls and streams so faithfully that to gaze at it gives the impression of being in a peaceful spot very remote from any human habitation.

Many Japanese live surrounded by nature, and are very dependent upon it. Their houses are built to hoard the warmth of the sun in winter and the cooling airs in summer. Every morning, in all seasons, a Japanese typically throws open one side of the room to let in the healthful air, and crouches at the sill to contemplate his tiny garden, the very puddles of which are treasured. The blast in winter serves to strengthen him, the sunshine in spring to warm him and the summer air to cool him. His garden is an object of contemplation, like the flower arrangement and work of art in his *tokonoma* (the alcove where every inch of precious space is used to best advantage by the simple artistic placing of two or three objects). He might even be inspired by this contemplation to compose a haiku like the following by Hackett:

Two flies, so small
it's a wonder they ever met,
are mating on this rose.

One rose with its attendant flies—such are the subjects of his meditation. He feels himself one with nature, and frees himself from likes and dislikes—not in the sense of being indifferent, but in the sense of finding meaning in all things. Putting aside the concept of ugliness, unpleasant and disgusting things become interesting and meaningful.[16] In this spirit, a certain eminent university professor in Tokyo finds relaxation in cleaning out drains around his house and even in cleaning his cat's ears. Freedom from creeds, general statements and ideologies, living close to the mist and rain and letting creatures live in the same way—this is necessary for haiku. As early as the eighth century, the Japanese love for nature manifests itself in this poem from the *Manyoshu*, translated by Blyth:

In the days of spring the mountain is fair to see;
In autumn nights the waters are clear.
Together through the morning clouds fly the cranes;
In the mists the frogs are loud.[17]

It is difficult for English-speaking people to realize how close to nature the Japanese are and how this closeness affects social behaviour. Westerners know nothing of the ways in which Japanese homes allow nature to enter by every window and every crack—wintry blasts, flower seeds, views of the sky and trees, insects, reptiles, rodents, cricket songs—all remind man of his place in the order of nature.[18] The Taoist belief in the unity and harmony of all things, the Shinto animism and the Buddhist doctrine of the transmigration of souls create deep respect for animals and, indeed, for all beings. For the Japanese, all are fellow creatures which must be allowed their own freedom. It is for man to "ask nothing from them, to give them all the freedom and happiness consistent with their own existence,"[19] to enjoy them for their beauty and to write without condescension of their habits.

Basho is noted for his devotion to nature, which was for him what it was for Gerard Manley Hopkins, something to be loved and studied with humility. He writes:

Samidare wo
Atsumete hayashi
Mogami-gawa

Collecting all
The rains of May
The swift Mogami River.

In Japanese, *samidare* implies the rain of the long, late-spring rainy season. There are many synonyms for it, and its connotations conjure up many memories for a native of Japan. At the riverside, though sound is not mentioned, nature is so present that the river is heard and felt as well as seen.

Issa shows compassionate irony in his attitude towards a snail in his haiku:

> *Katatsumuri*
> *Sorosoro nobore*
> *Fuji no yama*

> O snail
> Climb Mount Fuji
> But slowly, slowly!

The creature is acting according to its nature, doing what it was made to do. Therefore it is exhorted to go slowly while aspiring to the sacred heights.

One of Hackett's best haiku is a simple picture of birds acting according to their nature:

> A bitter morning:
> sparrows sitting together
> without any necks.

Sparrows huddled thus are a common sight on a cold day. It is in their nature so to keep themselves warm.

For Zen believers man and nature are united. The aim of learning is to abolish the division between man and nature and between man and man. Haiku over and over again reflect this unity of man with man and of man with nature, this intuition of shared nature and kinship. Since man is in tune with nature, in writing of it the most important things may be left unsaid.

The corollary to love of nature is love of the ordinary. Zen is unabashed in speaking of such daily duties as washing, eating, sleeping. A fit subject for haiku and one which comes close to *senryu* has been *jinji* (human affairs), at least as early as Basho, and ever since. The Japanese, according to Blyth, "have (had) the same sense of the religiousness, the cosmic meaning of daily life, as the ancient Greeks. Passing over the threshold, rising in the morning, going to rest in the evening, entering into manhood, all had their own sacred ritual, their cheerful solemnity."[20] Zen is concerned neither with sin nor with virtuous action. Loving, responsive, free acceptance makes the poet good without being either moral or immoral. One arrives at morality through action; morality is not a point of departure, as in the West. There are no rules of morality in Zen. Each situation is to be met according to its particular circumstances, in peace, without worry, but with concentrated attention. The continual attitude of acceptance of all events, coupled with a deep response to all creatures, generates a great freedom of action.

Just as Blake saw "a World in a grain of sand," so
the Japanese are interested in small and humble things.
They live in a country where everyone, merely by
climbing a nearby mountain, can obtain a view of the
ocean, of towering peaks or of innumerable round
hills which have seemingly bubbled up from some
not-too-ancient pot of boiling lava; yet, perhaps be-
cause their living quarters are confined to narrow val-
leys, they love small things. They make a hobby of
constructing small furniture and exceedingly small
scenes carved in walnut shells or from peach stones.
They love to observe the minute things of nature—
tiny plants, insects, fish. They understand the potter's
wheel and they prize hand-made cups of dark-brown
glossy ceramics as much as they prize oil paintings.
Household utensils, whether of clay, metal or rushes,
are all artistically made. It is no wonder, then, that
the eye of the Japanese haiku poet is accustomed to
notice the beauty of everyday things, and to find
meaning in everyday actions. On the school stage,
when the young actor successfully imitates the ordi-
nary action of his father drinking sakè, the audience
applauds. It is natural that eyes focused to see the in-
trinsic value of all things, small or great, should help
the haiku master to find meaning in everyday things.

The Zen-lover finds that we are too much in earnest
about things. We cannot find the ultimate reality be-
cause we are looking for it in obscure places when all

the time, as Alan Watts has pointed out, it is right out in broad daylight.[21] Zen has the common sense to see what is in front of everyone's nose. It does not, like Wordsworth (who, fortunately, did not follow his own advice), try to cast an aura of romance over common everyday things, but simply brings attention to the object, confident that it will manifest its nature adequately to the sensitive receiver. Zen does not even stretch out to nature. It does not have the vice of self-consciousness, of watching oneself experience things. A poet of Basho's calibre creates in himself a vacuum to draw in all the beauties of nature as well as the beauties of ordinary things. The following is by Basho:

> *Shiodai no*
> *Haguki mo samushi*
> *Uo no tana*

> In the fish-shop
> The gums of the salt bream
> Look cold.

Even in things so ordinary and repulsive as fish gums Basho finds poetry. In this haiku there are no values of pretty or ugly—just the peculiar being of the fish. In the original Japanese, the words *shiodai* and *samushi* bring to the ear the faraway clash of waves on the shore. The *o* and *a* sounds emphasize the sadness and the cold.

In English haiku there are examples of the use of everyday things as subjects. Hackett has written,

> Sweeping into a pan:
> the narrow line of dust
> that defies its edge.

This is an experience of *jinji* felt by anyone who has ever used a broom and dustpan. The line of dust is anthropomorphized and made to defy the dustpan. The number of times the action has to be repeated, the inevitable lack of entire success as the ever-diminishing line never quite completely enters the pan, convey to the sweeper a sense of the age-old continuity of a rhythm of life—the daily sweeping which, like the daily cooking, must always be begun anew. Hackett understands the value of everyday actions and things, the common sense of things. Although the average modern Westerner lacks this taste for everyday things, it is not unknown to Western writers. Henry Thoreau is a case in point. Describing the shanty of a neighbour, and the house in which he lived at Walden Pond, he writes:

> The roof was the soundest part, though a good deal warped and made brittle by the sun. Doorsill there was none, but a perennial passage for the hens under the doorboard.

* * *

I built the chimney after my hoeing in the fall, before a fire became necessary for warmth, doing my cooking in the meanwhile out of doors on the ground early in the morning.[22]

Even to the outdoor cooking early in the morning, this corresponds to Japanese taste for everyday actions and objects. There is meaning for Zen in ordinary objects and actions which (again let it be noted) are presented without comment.

ZEN AND THE WEST

At this point the question might be asked: Can Western man understand Zen, permeated as he is with Christian teaching? The answer is that Christ's teaching is not incompatible with Zen.

A university student while visiting Gasan asked him: "Have you ever read the Christian Bible?" "No, read it to me," said Gasan. The student opened the Bible and read from St. Matthew: "And why take ye thought for raiment? Consider the lilies of the field, how they grow. They toil not, neither do they spin, and yet I say unto you that even Solomon in all his glory was not arrayed like one of these. . . . Take therefore no thought for the morrow, for the morrow shall take thought for the things of itself."

Gasan said: "Whoever uttered those words I consider an enlightened man."

The student continued reading: "Ask and it shall be given you, seek and ye shall find, knock and it shall be opened unto you. For everyone that asketh receiveth, and he that seeketh findeth, and to him that knocketh, it shall be opened."

Gasan remarked: "That is excellent. Whoever said that is not far from Buddhahood."[23]

From the mouth of a Zen teacher, in this story transcribed by Shinzaki Nyogen and Paul Reps, Christian teaching is declared to be close to Buddhism.

Christ, as man, is the model for all Christians. If his life and teachings evidence the Zen spirit, it may be presumed that Christianity is not incompatible with Zen. And indeed, the life and teachings of Christ do illustrate much of what has been said so far. Christ, like Hakuin, is detached yet kind. His is a strength tempered by gentleness, a gravity saved by humour, a sympathy mingled with joy, an intelligence illumined by simplicity. He is *the* man par excellence, the one whom Buddhists would call a Buddha, as well as the one whom Christians consider to be the perfect man.

The Asiatic-Semitic aspects of Christ's teaching are paradoxical in that Christ is detached and compassionate at the same time. This is excellently illustrated in the incident with the Canaanite woman (Mark 7:24–

31) where Jesus shows detachment by at first rebuking her, saying that it is not right to take the children's bread and give it to the dogs, but shows compassion by later praising her for her words. The Zen qualities examined earlier all belong to Christ. Directness is illustrated by the Beatitudes (Matt. 5:3–12), which are, incidentally, favourite gospel texts in Japan. Christ is in his life intuitive, open to events and, above all, loving, as so many passages in scripture show—that of the Canaanite mentioned already, the good Samaritan parable, his weeping over Jerusalem and his love for Lazarus and Mary Magdalen, to mention a few. Christ often used paradox, for example when he said that he who finds his life will lose it (Matt. 11:39).

Austerity with its attendant detachment, simplicity and silence are evidenced in Christ's life as an artisan and in his later wandering life. Joy is shown by his attendance at weddings and feasts to such an extent that the Pharisees complain that his disciples do not fast. Gusto and earthiness are found in his examples, which vividly demand attention. He asks people if they do not realize that whatever enters the mouth passes into the belly and is cast out into the privy (Matt. 15:17). Christ, as an Asiatic in a warm country, lives out-of-doors, close to nature. Many of his examples are drawn from nature. As an artisan he is also aware of his tools, of the things used in everyday life—mustard seeds, money (groats and talents), of occupations like sheep herding and wheat sowing, grape raising and wine making.

Although Christ gives sermons, he detests sermonizing and hypocritical cant, which he denounces in the Pharisees just as the Zen monks oppose the Tantrics. Christ is against formalism, as he is against sentimentality, for he does not hesitate to berate the "whited sepulchres." His Zen attitudes, although distorted, submerged and overlaid, in time, with a burden of philosophical thought, are still a part of the European heritage, there in Biblical literature for the poet to find.

In the examples of English haiku given, there are usually non-haiku elements. Yet, on the whole, enough understanding of Zen is evidenced to lead to the conclusion that haiku composition is not impossible to Westerners. Biblical literature may be, for many, the best bridge to Zen.

Having examined the haiku moment, as well as the conditions for Zen *satori* and for the haiku moment, we may conclude that Zen and haiku in their many aspects, particularly in their closeness to nature and complete openness to life, are not necessarily antipathetic to Western conditions. Human nature has always reacted to the moments in which time seems to stand still and other considerations drop away, as some ordinary object becomes invested with a peculiar significance. The haiku moment is a universal experience.

IV | THE THREE-LINE FORM

It has been seen that the haiku moment and the Zen qualities of haiku have been experienced and expressed in English. It remains to examine, first in Japanese and then in English, the forms and techniques used by poets who have written successful haiku. These techniques to a certain extent will be seen to correspond to the Zen qualities examined in the previous chapter. To love of the ordinary corresponds the plain word; to the love of nature corresponds the use of the season word. These will be examined in subsequent chapters. To directness and austerity corresponds the brevity of the three-line form. This will be investigated here under three headings: the 17 syllables, the 5–7–5 arrangement and the methods of achieving brevity and concision. The possibilities of four- and two-line forms will be investigated through an examination of various translations of famous haiku. In this study of technique, the criterion of judgment will be the suitability of form to expression.

The Seventeen Syllables

In Japanese, 17 syllables is the ideal number for haiku. According to Kenneth Yasuda, "the intent of all haiku and the discipline of the form"[1] is to render the haiku moment, to express the "ah-ness." By physical necessity, the duration of the state of "ah-ness" is the length of a breath. The moment of union, of "ah-ness," of intuition and concentration of the mind lasts one breath,

> for as the poet exhales, that in itself draws the haiku moment to its close, and his vision is completed. Consequently, to form the experience, the length of the line for a haiku thought must have the same length as a breath's length. . . .[2]

By the one-breath poem "the true image of beauty . . . as it was experienced by the poet"[3] is re-created in the mind of the reader. A haiku by Buson quoted above illustrates this:

> *Botan chitte*
> *Uchikasanarinu*
> *Nisanpen*

> The peony has fallen
> A few scattered petals
> Lie one on another.

The sudden action of the falling petals is echoed in the brevity of the one-breath, four-word Japanese poem. R. H. Blyth, among others, also regards 17 syllables as the desired length for "one emission of breath, one exhalation of soul."[4] The one-breath poem re-creates in the mind of the reader the insight into the beauty of nature and the aesthetic pleasure of the haiku moment.

The number of syllables to express a breath-length haiku in English need not necessarily be the same as in Japanese. Indeed, it must be stressed that the two languages are very different. English has a widely varying accentual weight, both within the word and within the sentence pattern. Japanese in its polysyllabic words is almost without accent. As Mario Pei has explained,

> There is no strong stress in Japanese, the syllables of a word being about equally stressed. *Yokohama* is pronounced *Yókóhámá*, not *Yokoháma*. A certain amount of stress falls on long vowels, as well as on vowels followed by double consonants. Within the sentence, case particles, or postpositions, are specially stressed, which gives the Japanese sentence a rhythm completely foreign to western ears, but not too unlike that which schoolboys erroneously impart to Latin when they recite paradigms (*murús, muri, muró*, etc., instead of *múrus, múri, múro*).[5]

According to Pei, Japanese is spoken much more quickly than English, averaging 310 syllables a minute to the English 220.[6] Yet, different as English is from Japanese, Yasuda has given the following examples to show that a breath-length of poetry in English is about 17 syllables:

> Under yonder beech-tree single on the greensward,
> Couched with her arms behind her golden hair. . .
>
> —GEORGE MEREDITH

> It was many and many a year ago
> In a kingdom by the sea.
>
> —EDGAR ALLAN POE

The first quotation, containing 22 syllables, is much longer than a breath. The second, of 18 syllables, can be read easily in one breath. Other instances demonstrate that, in English as well as Japanese, depending on the diction, about 17 syllables is the usual number which can be read in one breath. Nevertheless it is important to remember that the syllables of the English language are of varying length and difficulty of pronunciation. This has been illustrated by Harold G. Henderson, who quotes contrasting 5-syllable phrases by Pope: "some huge stones, vast, white . . ." and "a little pebble."[8] It has also been shown by R. H. Blyth, who has contrived a verse to demonstrate how very long 17 syllables can be in English.

In a potato
Those groans whose forced prayers change nought,
Can never occur.[9]

English monosyllables can be very difficult to pro-
nounce, as the Renaissance poet Thomas Campion
recognized when he wrote, "Our English monosyl-
lables enforce many breathings which no doubt greatly
lengthen a verse."[10] Yet the attempt to Latinize Eng-
lish has never been completely successful among poets,
who recognize and love the power of the Anglo-Saxon
inheritance. The abundance of monosyllables in Eng-
lish, in contrast to the numerous polysyllabic words in
Japanese, makes for a larger word-count in English
haiku. Whereas the average Japanese haiku contains
only 5 or 6 words, the average English haiku runs to
12 or 13, omitting articles. Yet Yasuda, Blyth and
Henderson seem to agree with Hackett that the 17-
syllable count should be used if possible, although it
cannot be strictly adhered to. A solution to the diffi-
culty of overly long English haiku would be to use an
approximation of the Japanese method of counting
syllables. The Japanese syllabication is explained by
Henderson:[11] long vowels are written as two units, as
in *shóshó*, which is not 2 syllables but 4, *sho-o-sho-o*;
nasal *n* is counted as a separate syllable; a doubled con-
sonant, as it always entails a pause similar to that in the
English "rat-tail," is counted 2; for example, *ippun*
(one minute) is written as 4 syllables, i-p-pu-n. There

is no strictly logical reason for these rules. As in all
languages, the rules simply exist.

If a Japanese student were asked to memorize J. W.
Hackett's sparrow poem,

> A bitter morning:
> sparrows sitting together
> without any necks.

he might write it for his own convenience in the Japa-
nese phonetic alphabet. In that case it would be ex-
panded to

> A bi-ta mo-o-ni-n-gu
> su-pa-ro-o-zu shi-chi-n-gu tsu-ge-za-a
> u-i-zu-a-u-to e-ni ne-ku-su.

By reading this very quickly, the student would ap-
proximate the English original. Thus, even short Eng-
lish haiku are overly long by Japanese standards.

Naturally, it would be impossible to attempt total
use of the Japanese method of counting syllables in
English, but writers of English haiku would do well
to keep in mind the extreme brevity of the Japanese
form. In view of this, it is suggested that at least Eng-
lish consonant clusters and long accented vowels be
counted as 2 syllables. Punctuation, if any, should also
be included in the syllable count. If the English long

vowels and slowing consonants, such as the *pl* and *ow* in "plow," were counted as 2 syllables each, as they are in Japanese, there could be little doubt that 17 syllables is the best length for English haiku.

THE 5–7–5 ARRANGEMENT

The arrangement of the 17 syllables into three lines in the 5–7–5 pattern gives proportion and symmetry. As has been noted, the haiku moment is an instant of unity and harmony with nature. This, writes Yasuda, requires to be expressed in a "unified, well-ordered whole corresponding with the insight."[12] Just as the intuition produces understanding of proportions and values, so its expression should be balanced and harmonious.

There are usually three elements in any haiku, one for each line, telling the where, the when and the what of the haiku moment. The classic example, below, is by Basho:

> *Kare eda ni*
> *Karasu no tomari keri*
> *Aki no kure*

> On a leafless bough
> A crow is perched—
> The autumn dusk.

In the first line the place is located, in the second the object in nature is identified and in the third the season is introduced. The balance and symmetry of short-long-short in this poem are suited to its intensity. In each haiku there is a special pause or turning, either after the 5th or after the 12th syllable, which is not so much a thought-pause as a sense-pause dictated by aesthetic necessity, perhaps reflecting the asymmetry of nature's artistry, as the odd number of lines and syllables in each line does. In the crow poem, the pause comes after the second line; in the frog poem it is after the first line. The turning reinforces the necessity of the 5–7–5 arrangement. (According to Penny Scribner,[13] the 5–7–5 form illustrates four other artistic principles: balance, in the grouping of two shorter lines against a longer; repetition, in the 5-syllable lines; variety or artistic asymmetry, by the inclusion of the 7-syllable line; and unity, in the neat, compact poem which calls for precision and purposefulness.) Hence, in Japanese, the 5–7–5 arrangement is the most usual and the most suitable, although there are exceptions.

The observations made concerning the balance, proportion, symmetry and asymmetry, the three elements and the turning of Japanese haiku may apply also to English. It should be noted that there is a general tradition in English verse which runs strongly contrary to the haiku form; nevertheless the remarks about the 5–7–5 arrangement do apply to successful English haiku such as Hackett's sparrow poem. If syllables are counted in English in the way recommended earlier, there is no reason why the 5–7–5 arrangement should not be suitable to English as well as Japanese haiku, keeping in mind that approximate equivalence may often be sufficient.

How Brevity Is Achieved

"Pregnancy and suggestiveness, brevity and ellipsis are the soul and life of a haiku."[14] Brevity in Japanese haiku depends upon three things: the structure of the language, the poem's confinement to a moment and the place of haiku in a continuing poetic tradition. The structure of the language permits much compression because pronouns are seldom used and verbs are often employed in the brief infinitive form. When expanded, as they may be in many ways, they acquire great richness, as Joseph K. Yamagiwa explains in relation to the verb *sumu*:

> . . . the forms *sumeri, sumitari, suminu, sumiki* and *sumikeri*, all based on the verb *sumu*, to live, may each be rendered in the past suffix, as in *sumitari-keru* or *sumerishi*. With such a system of inflections, it is easily possible to compose an entire five- or seven-syllable line with a form based on a single verb.[15]

These numerous inflected suffixes, he continues, "express extremely subtle distinctions of mood." This richness of inflection allows Japanese haiku to contain only 4 or 5 words, as contrasted with English haiku, which usually include 11 or 12. Adjectives in Japanese are capable of being used in an elliptical form as prefixes attached to the nouns they modify, as has been noted in the case of *furui* (old) which becomes *furu* when attached to *ike* (pond). There are no Japanese equivalents for the English articles "a" and "the." Nouns are seldom differentiated as singular or plural. Particles are brief postpositions indicating case, which, when used in haiku, may impart strong emotional meaning. The many homonyms provide an echoing depth of meaning unknown in European languages.

The problem of the English haiku poet is how to achieve brevity harmoniously with the effects, devices and elements of the English language. Yasuda recommends the use of unaccented syllables, liquid sounds and polysyllabic words to counteract the differences in language.[16] English too can be elliptical, punctuation often replacing parts of speech, as in Hackett's poem, "Sweeping into a pan:" in which the colon has a meaning which would probably be expressed by *ya* in Japanese, as will be seen later. Unfortunately, however, there is a growing tendency on the part of poor craftsmen to use unnatural ellipsis in English. Even Yasuda is not free from this fault. His translation of the crow poem is an example:

> On a withered bough
> A crow alone is perching
> Autumn evening now.

For the sake of rhyme he uses the unnatural ellipsis of the last line.

Haiku poets also achieve brevity by confining themselves to the expression of the haiku moment. Thus, according to Scribner,[17] the artistic principle of dominance requires the poet to set a mood and to repudiate all words which do not contribute to the purpose. Haiku poets writing in English would do well to pay the greatest attention to this principle, taking care to have each word contribute its full share to the meaning while pruning away any which do not aid in the expression of the flash of insight. Ichiki Tadao, speaking of the essential brevity of haiku, emphasizes the importance of ellipsis; he compares the pause to "+ and —in electricity separated by a gap." Just as the "spark" leaps over the space, so "the mind must make a leap" to bridge the gap between the "two apparently different or unrelated ideas."[18] The ellipsis is, then, not only a matter of form, but a meaningful force. (Blake's short poems illustrate this same principle.) Earl Miner, defending brief forms of poetry, remarks that the Japanese (who are willing to sit through dramas which last for days) have received poetic satisfaction from short poems since prehistoric times. He accounts for this partly by the fact that a good haiku has a secure place in a continuing poetic tradition. "Japanese poetry is a continuing body of tradition, conventions, and assumptions between poets and readers unlike anything in Western poetry."[19] However, the actual techniques of imagery, verbal and syntactical dexterity and use of literary allusion are not essentially different from Western use. The difference is in the degree of concentration rather than the techniques. In time, a similar tradition of concentration could grow up in English.

Two- and Four-line Haiku

Some haiku translators, especially early ones, have used two-, four- or even one-line forms.

> Collecting all the rains of May,
> How swiftly flows the Mogami!
>
> [MIYAMORI]

> How swiftly move
> The June rains
> Brought together
> In the Mogami River!
>
> [S. H. WAINRIGHT]

> With all the waters of the season's rain
> The Mogami doth rush into the main.
>
> [S. NISHIMURA]

Of these three poems, the first is the best, yet the "how" is a comment. The second is too clever, with its concept of the rains moving. The third lacks the haiku spirit of immediacy. A comparison of these translations with the following version by Blyth shows his to be superior.

> Collecting all
> The rains of May
> The swift Mogami River.

No statement is needed, nor even a principal verb. The poem has the power of resonance, given strength by its concision. Of the recent translators, few recommend quatrains for haiku. But Yuasa Nobuyuki, who translated several of Basho's travel diaries in 1966, uses four-line stanzas, giving three reasons for his choice. "First, the language of haiku . . . is based on colloquialism, and in my opinion, the closest approximation of natural conversational rhythm can be achieved in English by a four-line stanza rather than a constrained three-line stanza." In other words, the four-line stanza gives the desired colloquial conversational rhythm. He continues. "Second, even in the lifetime of Basho, *hokku* . . . was given a special place in the series and treated half-independently, and in my opinion a three-line stanza does not carry adequate dignity and weight. "

This is, in effect, the chief criticism of haiku in English—that is, that it is too light, too brief. It is the work of English poets to overcome this fault. Perhaps Yuasa has the solution, but general practice disagrees with him. He continues: "Finally, I had before me the task of translating a great number of poems mixed with prose, and I found it impossible to use [the] three-line form consistently."[20] Most haiku writers in English would agree that it is difficult to use the three-line form consistently. This does not mean, however, that it is not to be regarded as the recommended ideal. Yuasa's translations are interesting to examine as examples of four-line haiku:

Furu ike ya
Kawazu tobikomu
Mizu no oto

Breaking the silence
Of an ancient pond
A frog jumped into water—
A deep resonance.

Apart from the fact that "a deep resonance" is not the meaning of *mizu no oto*, and the original does not mention the silence, this dignified translation does not faithfully convey the lightness of sound of the original. It is rewarding to compare translations by Blyth and Yuasa:

> Nothing intimates,
> In the voice of the cicada,
> How soon it will die.

> Hardly a hint
> Of their early death
> Cicadas singing
> In the trees.

Yuasa's use of strong Anglo-Saxon words, notably "hint," is not to be disparaged, but the Latinate polysyllabic "intimates" of Blyth's translation is even better in this case, given the demands of haiku. Here again Yuasa has added something—the phrase "in the trees" does not appear in the original. Other examples of familiar haiku translated by Yuasa are:

> The moment you open
> Your mouth to speak,
> The autumn wind stirs
> And chills your lips.

This is verbose enough to constitute two breath-lengths of poetry.

> The ancient poet
> Who pitied monkeys for their cries,
> What would he say, if he saw
> This child crying in the autumn wind?

In a commendable effort to convey the full meaning, Yuasa's translations add much comment not found in the originals. In a translation, this added comment is understandable. However, its consistent use does a disservice to English haiku. The meaning of the monkey haiku is rendered clearly, but this version does not successfully convey a haiku moment.

> *Samidare wo*
> *Atsumete hayashi*
> *Mogami-gawa*

> Gathering all the rains
> Of May,
> The River Mogami rushes down
> In one violent stream.

The break after "rains" gives an unwarranted emphasis to line two. The gentle impact of *samidare* (May rains) would probably be better communicated by a three-line arrangement:

> Gathering all the rains of May
> The River Mogami rushes down
> In one violent stream.

Nevertheless, the redundant last line makes the poem too long for haiku.

It has been alleged that the three-line stanza is foreign to English poetic expression. Yet the tradition in British poetry goes back at least as far as the famous poem by Robert Herrick on Julia's clothes, and in Wallace Stevens's collected poems there are no less than 1,245 three-line stanzas. An examination of a recently published volume of verse[21] discloses that 34 other poets made use of the three-line form. While not a startling figure in view of the total number of poets, it demonstrates that there is some precedent for the use of three-line stanzas. It is perhaps true that the quatrain sounds more familiar to the English ear. Yet it seems that the austere three-line stanza may provide a freshness and significance scarcely found today in the quatrain used for haiku.

Henderson agrees that there is a growing tendency to approximate the three-line, 5–7–5 form, but no experienced poet or editor holds to it strictly.[22] The form is the handmaid of the poem, not vice-versa. An examination of two- and three-line verse forms seems to indicate that the three-line form is generally the most suitable for haiku, as the following examples of "experiments in English," original haiku by Yasuda, may illustrate:

> The lizard flicks over
> The undulating ripples
> Of sunlit clover.

The choice of the polysyllabic "undulating" and the short-syllabled "sunlit" is particularly effective.

> Moving in one big sway
> The flowering winter peony
> Scatters bright and gay.

Reminiscent of Buson's famous peony poem, this is also effective word-painting.

> A crimson dragonfly,
> As it lights, sways together
> With a leaf of rye.

The choice of the disyllabic "crimson" and of the trisyllabic "dragonfly" and "together," as well as such short-vowelled words as "lights" and "leaf," is particularly fortunate.

The three-line poem in the form of 17 syllables, the 5–7–5 arrangement, and techniques for achieving brevity have been examined. The 17 syllables provide the breath-long expression needed to represent the haiku moment. The 5–7–5 grouping supplies artistic proportion, symmetry and asymmetry. It has been noted that the conditions and techniques for attaining brevity in the Japanese haiku are not inconsistent with similar conditions and techniques in English. Finally, the possibilities of the couplet and the quatrain as forms for haiku have been examined, and generally the three-line form has been seen to have advantages over the other forms. Perhaps Blyth presents the solution most suitable to the present stage in the evolution of English haiku:

> The haiku form is thus a simple and yet deeply "natural" form, compared to the sonnet, blank verse, and the other borrowed forms of verse in English. The ideal, that is, the occasionally attainable haiku form in English, would perhaps be three short lines, the second a little longer than the other two.[23]

The method of achieving the ideal line length might well be to count haiku syllables in English in a manner similar to the Japanese. At least an awareness of the Japanese method is valuable in encouraging greater flexibility in the writing of English haiku. Considering what has been said of the haiku form, it seems, therefore, that the direct, austere, three-line form of Japanese haiku is also the most suitable form for English haiku.

V | THE SEASON WORD

An integral element of most haiku, the season word, relates to Zen interest in nature. A brief history of the season word will be followed, in the present chapter, by an examination of its meaning and use and a survey of the chief season subjects used in Japanese and English haiku. Suggestions will be given for season topics in English haiku. Finally, to help clarify the function of the season word, its relationship to tone will be investigated and the phenomenon of the "death poem" will be briefly discussed.

HISTORY OF THE SEASON WORD

A brief reference, direct or indirect, to one of the seasons is an old tradition in Japanese poetry, and the contents of Japanese books of poetry are usually divided according to the season, with New Year's as a fifth season added to the traditional four.

Although the history of the season word in Japanese

poetry is long, the poems collected in the *Manyoshu* (eighth century) are not classified according to season. The seasonal division of poems was made in 905 for the first time, in the *Kokinshu* anthology. This seasonal division proved to be an enduring method of classifying poetry, and the season word is a seldom-overlooked part of *waka*. For Basho the season word is the most important element in haiku, since it provides a vehicle for situating an intuition. By concentrating seriously on natural objects he finds them to be microcosms reflecting the macrocosm of their seasonal background. In this century Kawahigashi Hekigodo (1873–1937) and others advocating freer haiku moved towards dropping the season word as well as the 5-7-5 form. However, an examination of haiku which contain no definite season word reveals that the total effect still indicates a particular season.

> *Ippon-bashi wo*
> *Kodomo ga kuru*
> *Inu ga kuru asa*

> With morning comes
> A child, then a dog
> Across the log bridge.

This haiku by Ogiwara Seisensui (b. 1884) indicates summer, as the Japanese syntax shows quite clearly in a more literal translation—"the kind of morning which brings a child and dog over the single-log bridge."

> *Yama wa hito no*
> *Sumu kemuri hitosuji no*
> *Aoi sora*

> A line of smoke rising
> Someone is living there in the mountains—
> The blue sky.

The total effect of this haiku, also by Seisensui, indicates autumn because of the conjunction of the clear blue sky and the smoke signalling a warming fire. Nakatsuka Ippekiro (1887–1946), another modern, pays no attention to the season word, which, if it is present, is not central. His point of view is different from that of earlier haiku writers.

> *Omoikiri hashitte*
> *Wakaba no yami e*
> *Haitte mo mitai*

> I feel like rushing
> Into the darkness
> Of the young leaves.

The central emotion of this poem is the great rushing

desire. The young leaves, although meaningful in that they seem to echo the youthfulness of the speaker, are yet peripheral. On the whole, however, the modern response to the attempt to drop the season word suggests the conviction that such freedom would destroy haiku. Kenneth Yasuda asserts that there should at least be a seasonal feeling, where a specific seasonal word would be lifelessly conventional.[1]

MEANING AND USE OF THE SEASON WORD

The season word provides a brief reference to the time of the year and suggests a whole background of imagery which greatly broadens the scope of the poem. Peter Beilenson calls the season word a shortcut, introducing the reader to a whole surrounding atmosphere of weather, to plants and trees, sights, sounds and smells, all of which are valuable elements in the poem.[2] The season word may be one of two important elements in a good haiku, which usually requires the juxtaposition of two concepts. In Basho's crow poem the whole background of the autumn evening is a general setting for the instant in time when the crow on the withered branch is perceived. According to Donald Keene, there must be a spark which leaps from one image to the other:[3] otherwise the poem is not a haiku but a mere statement of fact, and poetry deals not with facts, but with relationships.

The mention of the season is sometimes explicit, as in the crow poem, where the word "autumn" appears, sometimes implicit, as in the frog poem, where the presence of the frog implies that it is spring. Sometimes the season is mentioned not in one particular word, but in the pervasive feeling of the whole poem, as in the combined images of the autumn haiku by Seisensui quoted above:

> A line of smoke rising
> Someone is living there in the mountains—
> The blue sky.

Certain season words have quite absolute connotations. Any other use of them jars and frustrates. An example known even to children is *soyo kaze* (soft breeze) which may only be used in reference to spring, never to summer or autumn.

THE NEW YEAR SEASON, SPRING AND SUMMER

New Year's is the most solemn religious festival in Japan. All debts are paid, borrowed things returned, the house completely cleaned and decorated. The father blesses the assembled family, everyone receives new chopsticks and new clothing, all go to the temple at midnight to pray while the bell is rung 108 times to purify from the heart the 108 kinds of sin. The next morning at a special wine-drinking congratulatory ceremony, everyone in the family becomes one year older. According to Blyth, the mood of the day is that all things are new and fresh while remaining the same. New Year's morning is not only the morning of the day but the morning of the whole year. All things being renewed, man also is capable of reforming himself. Since the Japanese followed the old lunar calendar until quite recently, all their customs are in harmony with its pattern. Under the lunar calendar, New Year's occurs about the time which corresponds to early February. By then, spring is making itself felt. Plum blossoms appear in sheltered spots and there is more sunshine.[4] The word *ganjitsu* (New Year's Day) is the most important season word, bringing with it, perhaps, connotations even deeper than the word Christmas in the West. Poems are written about such things as the first dream, first water, first load, first sky of the New Year.

The Los Altos Writers have some haiku about Christmas, placed, naturally, in the winter section of their book.

> Christmas melts slowly
> in a home filled with children—
> there, love is solid.
>
> —JOY SHIEMAN[5]

It seems that there is too much philosophical statement in this poem. The last line is redundant, since the concept is understood from the first two lines. There is no clear image to focus the haiku moment.

> The tree seems lifeless
> yet the mistletoe prospers—
> a kiss for Christmas?
>
> —HELEN S. CHENOWETH

Rather resembling a syllogism, this seems to reflect preoccupation with material things and too much self-interest.

As yet, Christmas as a subject for haiku has scarcely been investigated. Yet it is foreseeable that if haiku in English becomes widespread, Christmas might be the fifth season of the West, as, indeed, the word "Christmastide" implies. Like the Japanese New Year, Christmas also, with its preparatory liturgical season of Advent which begins the new Church year and its celebration of a birth, signifies a new beginning, a new dawning of hope. A rich mine of religious and natural imagery, with connotations echoing back through the early Renaissance *lauda* (religious songs) and Francis of Assisi, through the prophets to the Old Testament accounts of the Creation and the Fall, is yet to be used to advantage by Western writers. Apart from these, the many household customs and articles associated with

Christmas—bells, trees, candles, carols—have great allusive potentiality. It seems that the traditional aspects of Christmas are more suitable for haiku than the modern commercialized abuses of the sacred season suggest.

As a season, spring shares with New Year's and Christmas the mood of newness, but with more emphasis on the returning warmth. Birds and blossoms are the favourite subjects. Spring is the season of birdsong, especially that of the *uguisu* (Japanese bushwarbler); like the plum blossom, it is one of the first signs of spring. People who live in centrally heated homes cannot imagine the joy evoked by these signs of spring. The plum blossom is frail and delicate in appearance, yet it blooms while the weather is still cold.[6] Since the time of Sugawara no Michizane, a renowned political exile who wrote a well-known poem about it, the plum tree has been associated with nostalgia for home. The range and variety of haiku about cherry blossoms are amazing. The word "flower" used by itself means cherry blossom. The camellia is another early spring flower. The blooms are red or white, resembling wild roses, the leaves glossy and dark, the branches beautifully shaped for flower arranging. The white blooms are especially dramatic against the green leaves.[7] Other subjects are the long day, warmth, tranquillity, the light of spring, spring snow, the hazy moon, the soft breeze, spring rain, remaining snow, snow melting, spring rivers, the Ise shrine, the doll festival, shell gathering, tilling, planting, silkworms, tea-picking, cats in love, frogs, butterflies, azaleas and rape-flowers.

Of the English haiku mentioned in the spring section of *Borrowed Water*, fourteen contain the word "spring" directly. As in the Japanese haiku, blossoms are a favourite topic, but apricot rather than plum or cherry blossoms are chosen. Nesting birds are emphasized rather than singing birds; seedlings in garden plots and butterflies are also popular. The whole perspective seems to be that of nature in cultivated suburbia rather than the untamed nature of the Japanese countryside.

The potentialities of spring as a subject for English haiku are unlimited. The joyous season of Eastertide with its emphasis on rebirth, the going down into the waters of Baptism, the old theme of Christ's harrowing of hell, the preparatory seasons of Septuagesima and Lent, which echo once again the notion of creation, the forty days until Ascension Day—all are so rich in association that Japanese Christians have been quick to publish haiku on these subjects in their newspapers. The rich variety of flora and fauna, climatic conditions, planting customs and holidays in the widespread areas of the English-speaking world all provide an infinite fund of topics for future haiku. It is foreseeable that each district may have its local haiku with explanatory notes for the uninitiated. Spring, as a beautiful season in any country, does not fail to add its quota of material for haiku. (Ottawa, in Canada, for example, offers its tulips.)

If the dominant mood of spring is renewal, that of summer is perhaps the power of the elements. Favourite summer subjects are the heat of the day, the cool of the evening, rain, the fields and mountains, the cuckoo, the peony and summer insects. Great poetry is found in the simple elemental contrast of heat and cool. The monotonous rain is considered to produce change in all things, even the hearts of men. The vastness of still summer fields and mountains foreshadows infinity and eternity. The cuckoo is a perfect subject for haiku, as its Japanese name, *hototogisu*, contains five musical syllables. It arrives deep in the mountains of Japan in early summer. Slightly smaller than a pigeon, it has a blood-red mouth and sings a melancholy note while flying at night. The peony is a proud flower, the glory of man and nature. Fireflies and cicadas are subjects for poetry in many lands, but the humourous and compassionate Zen treatment of fleas, lice, flies and mosquitoes is peculiar to Japan.[8] Other subjects are billowing clouds, summer storms, burning sunshine, the *bon* (All Souls) festival, fans, the midday nap, parasols and the song of the planters.

English haiku containing summer season-words have been written on a great variety of subjects. The word "summer" itself does not appear as often as "spring." Summer flowers are popular, but no bloom in particular seems to embody the season. The moon, forest fires, insects, gulls and grain are mentioned. Such things as lawnmowers, garden hoses and picnics give a Western flavour.

The possibilities of summer in the northern sections of the English-speaking world have scarcely been looked into. In Canada, artists have painted objects of nature with haiku-like concentration. The local colour in their works might prove to be a source of fresh insight for haiku poets. In the liturgical cycle, the colourful feasts of Pentecost and Corpus Christi fall in the summer. These, as well as the sights and sounds of the city in summer, the fish of the fresh-water lakes, the hardy animals of the conifer forests, the northern lights, the cold night air and the taste and feel of spring-fed lake water all suggest further topics for haiku. The nightingale of England would bring to haiku a rich classical allusion, in addition to a seasonal element.

AUTUMN AND WINTER

Autumn, like summer, offers its quota of natural symbols. Both Japanese and English haiku share the autumn moon and falling leaves as their chief season words of autumn. In Japanese poetry "moon" alone refers to the autumn moon. According to Blyth, "the fall of the year is not merely the fall of the leaves but the fall of the vital powers in all natural things, including man."[9] The autumn wind brings the thought of death with it.[10] Scarecrows, formerly a peculiarly Japanese subject, are now being written about in America. The song of insects is a very popular subject. The Japanese claim that on autumn nights the insect orchestra has as many as twelve or thirteen different instruments, a fact which testifies to the acute training of the Japanese ear. The chrysanthemum, of which there are many varieties, is the outstanding autumn flower as well as the symbol of the imperial family. Other subjects are the cold, lengthened night, the milky way, lanterns, the charcoal kiln, visiting graves, the fulling block, gleaning, wrestling, medicinal roots, gourds, persimmons, apples and vines.

English haiku in addition stress the departure of birds. The note of sadness is mitigated in Western poetry by the aura of Thanksgiving. Autumn plenty, pumpkins, doves, crickets and logs for the fireplace—all reflect the more joyful, prosperous atmosphere to be expected of a young, affluent culture.

> South-bound roaring past
> splintering the night with sound—
> listen! a cricket.
>
> —ANNE RUTHERFORD

In the midst of the deafening sound of a fast train, the

clear cry of a cricket can be heard. Heedless prosperity and natural cheerfulness are juxtaposed in a haiku which properly expresses the insight of a modern person.

Further suggested topics for English haiku might be Indian Summer with all its vivid colours, the gold and black of the prairie fields, flaming maples, geese, the whirr of pheasants, the opening of school with its accompanying smells of varnish, wax and new books and, in the liturgical cycle, the feasts of Christ the King, All Saints and the feast the West shares with Japan, although the West celebrates it in autumn— All Souls. (The Hallowe'en festivities of the Occident bear a resemblance to the *bon* [All Souls] dances of Japan.) Early autumn is cheerful but, as the season wears on towards winter, the thought of death becomes more pressing.

Winter is not quite so much the season of death as might be thought, for it is permeated with the hope that spring is coming, rather in the spirit of Shelley's "O, Wind, / If Winter comes, can Spring be far behind?" As might be expected, snow is the favourite season-word for winter in both Japanese and English haiku. Winter is the season of the much-feared "great cold," which is not only a physical cold, but also a psychological numbness connected with fear and loneliness.[11] According to Blyth, "snow in winter corresponds in its range of significance and variety of treatment to the cherry blossoms of spring, the *hoto-togisu* in summer, the moon in autumn. Fields and mountains, when the trees are leafless and thickets are a wild tangle of browns and greys, have a poetic meaning that the green of the other seasons does not know."[12] Comparatively few haiku are written about winter animals; of the plants, fallen leaves are best handled. Other subjects are the depth of winter, the god-less month (that is, October, when the gods are meeting in Izumo), the withered moor, the dried-up waterfall, bowl-beating (a religious begging ceremony), failing strength, charcoal fire, banked fire, *kotatsu* (fire under a blanket-covered table), socks drying, the old calendar, and *mochi*-makers (makers of festive rice-cakes).

These subjects lean heavily towards human affairs. In English winter haiku too, menus (often including hot soup, wine or grape jelly), mention of furniture (clocks, rocking-horses, vases) show the indoor orientation of the people, but with great cultural difference of emphasis.

> All New England
> in a glass of wild grape jelly
> and a clambake.
>
> —CHENOWETH

This was included in the miscellaneous section and indeed it is difficult to classify, for it has two words indicating different seasons—clambake for summer and jelly for autumn.

> Twin pomegranates
> for my ancient bronze pitcher—
> how cross the jays are.
>
> —CATHERINE NEIL PATON

Included in the winter section of *Borrowed Water*, this depicts a warm southern winter, far from the numbing misery (at least for the poor) of Tokyo's *daikan* (literally, "great cold"). English haiku can, however, show insight into harsh nature.

> The cold winter wind
> writes its messages in shivers
> on the drifting snow.
>
> —GEORGIAN TASHJIAN

This description of hard-packed snow sculptured into ridges or "shivers" by a biting wind gives evidence of the author's keen eye for nature.

Material for further English haiku might include such things as continental winter blizzards, the sound of snow crunching underfoot, the stroking of skates on ice, mufflers on children, ski tracks and bird tracks in the snow, icicles, stark trees and evergreens, the warmth, colour and sound of an open fireplace, shovelling snow and sprinkling ashes. The dominant mood of English winter haiku should perhaps be the joy of struggling and winning over the harsh but attractive rigours of nature in the north.

TONE

Whether it indicates New Year's, Christmas, spring, summer, autumn or winter, the season word is perhaps most important for the contribution it makes to tone. As has been indicated, certain words produce a built-in response. In the hands of a poor versifier this is dangerous, but, like the formulae of the Anglo-Saxon and other European minstrels, in the hands of a good poet these words work magic. Plum blossoms or beasts of battle—both evoke a reaction in the accustomed hearer and both contribute to tone.

There are also certain technical terms applied to haiku which are related to tone and style. In addition to *wabi* and *sabi*, which have been mentioned in Chapter 1 in connection with the concept of loneliness, Blyth names *yugen, ushin, shiori, hosomi* and *shibumi*. It was seen that, although *wabi* refers to the beauty of old, worn things, and *sabi* is also something given by time, *sabi* is not found in the subject of the verse but in the flavour of it. As for the other terms, at the outset it must be stated that they deserve a much fuller treatment than it is possible to give them in this work, and that they are extremely difficult to explain. They are best understood by the senses, using analogies from painting and design. All are related to the central concept that the Absolute is found in nature. When Western man sees a beautiful scene he may praise God the Creator, or His immensity and omnipotence. The Japanese see nature as a reflection of God, as containing the Absolute. Their nature worship even influences their ethical judgments, causing them to use the naturally beautiful rather than the just as a criterion of good. Yet perfection in art is not to be expected, because perfection in a man-made work is a challenge to the almighty power, a mockery of the gods. That is why an artist who worked at the great shrine of Nikko deliberately included a blemish in his work as an admission of human weakness.

With these preliminary remarks in mind, it may be said that *yugen* implies religious mystery, profundity, subtlety and asceticism. Perhaps the closest English equivalent is "the numinous," which is defined as "that element in the religious object (the holy) and in religious feeling (consciousness of the holy) which is characteristic of all vital religion, moral or non-moral; the awe and awe-inspiring quality associated with religion and deity" (*Webster's Dictionary, Unabridged*). It is expressed in art, especially in the Noh drama, by an effortless artistry which is achieved when the essence, the core of the action or thing to be expressed, is reached, and the consequent expression, as a result, reflects the deepest, most profound meaning. The more the art of haiku or Noh is mastered, the greater the likelihood of expressing *yugen*; likewise, the more an experiencer understands the art, the greater the possibility of experiencing *yugen* in a work of art.

The numinous, the *yugen* in poetry provides *ushin*. When the word *ushin* refers to the feelings of the poet it may be translated as "sincerity." When *ushin* refers to the poem it might be translated "transcendental beauty." Perhaps the closest word in English is "sincerity," as used in criticism to indicate a work which is not sentimental and which makes no false pretences or undue claims for itself. Again, "forthrightness" might be the word. *Shiori* may come from *shioreru* (to wither, to droop), or from *shioru* (to bend). In any case, it is generally used to describe small, delicate things having a certain simple charm like the attraction of violets and anonymous field flowers. It seems to imply restraint in the use of poetic diction and devices, as well as in the choice of imagery. "Unpretentiousness" is perhaps the best equivalent English word. *Hosomi* (slenderness, or spareness), which is an aid to the attainment of *yugen*, seems to be applied to thought and diction. An equivalent English word might be "underemphasis." *Shibumi* (astringency), which gives a dark yet not unpleasant effect, like the shadowed effect in Rembrandt's paintings, calls for a severe, refined style as opposed to flamboyance or emotionalism. Perhaps "asceticism" is the nearest English equivalent. On the other hand, *aware* (the quality of arousing compassion) is much prized in haiku. The rare word "compassionable" is probably the nearest equivalent of *aware* in English. Japanese poetry, it has been stated, may be numinous, sincere, unpretentious, underemphatic, ascetic and compassionable. These adjectives are rather unfamiliar in modern aesthetics but, upon reflection, it may be noted that they are not entirely foreign as attributes of modern poetry.

English haiku in general have, so far, little *wabi, sabi* or *yugen*. They may be *aware* (compassionable) and *shibumi* (underemphatic), in their many contrasts between nature and mechanized or destructive society.

> Machines uprooted
> blossoming apricot trees.
> Progress never weeps.
> —CHENOWETH

Aware is present in the contrasting image of trees and machine. Apart from the redundant third line and the enjambment, this is good haiku.

> Hollowed charred tree stumps
> denied their part of living . . .
> now bees make honey.
> —CHENOWETH

The first line is much too long, although, strictly speaking, it contains only five syllables. The second line is unnecessary. The interesting juxtaposed images would be even more suitable material for haiku if handled with *shibumi*.

THE DEATH POEM

Loneliness, death and sickness are frequent elements in haiku. There may be a historical reason for this in the fact that for five centuries after the Heian period (794–1185) the country was ravaged, especially by civil wars between the Heike and Genji clans (1100–1219). The final sea battle in the Strait of Shimonoseki is a popular subject for song and story, as the tale "Earless Hoichi" testifies. An equivalent in English might be the battle of Culloden Moor. The Japanese claim that haiku are written when one is bored and lonely, not when happy or busy. A poem by Ishida Hokyo (1913–1969) supports this theory.

> *Ori no washi*
> *Sabishiku nareba*
> *Hautsu ka mo*

> The caged eagle;
> When lonely
> He flaps his wings.

To relieve his boredom, the eagle does something—
he flaps his wings; a man might write a poem. Lafcadio
Hearn discovered that "the old Japanese teaching is
that literary composition is the best medicine for sor-
row; . . . even among the poorest classes, poems are
still composed upon all occasions of joy or pain."[13]
This holds true today, in the second half of the twen-
tieth century. It is an admirable act to compose a poem
on one's death-bed. Basho, when asked for a farewell
poem, replied that every poem since his frog haiku
had been a farewell poem, as they were all written in
the same style and with the same attitude towards life.
Another death poem is the following by Naito Mei-
setsu (1847–1926):

> *Tada tanomu*
> *Yutampo hitotsu no*
> *Samusa kana*

> All I ask of you,—
> A hot-water bottle:
> The cold!

This farewell haiku illustrates Zen humour and
austerity.

Many poems, like this one by the modern poet
Hatsutaro, are written about death and sickness.

> *Ochiba michi*
> *Yuki todomarite*
> *Yama no haka*

> The path of fallen leaves
> Leads to the graves on the hill,
> And stops there.

The fallen leaves in this poem intensify the fact of the finality of the grave.

> *Byoin e*
> *Yuku byonin ni*
> *Hosoki kokage*

> The sick man
> Going to the doctor's,
> Slender tree-shadows on him.

The comparison of the slender tree shadows and the sick man heightens the effect of the man's weakness in the preceding haiku, composed by the modern poet Kafugen:

> *Kiri wo kishi*
> *Mo no shiro-tabi wo*
> *Nugi ni keri*

Come through the mist,
She took off the white tabi
Of her mourning clothes.

As white is the colour of mourning in Japan, the mist
and white socks are appropriate in a haiku about death,
written by the modern poet Maneishi.

The old ones pondered
A pale lemon winter sun
and bitter fruit.

—PEGGY CARD

Aware and *shibumi* are found in this poem, as the im-
plication is, of course, that the old people are also
pondering, by transferred epithet, pale, bitter sickness
and death.

Beside a new grave . . .
burdened with the crushing weight
of ungiven love.

—J. W. HACKETT

Two leaning tombstones
took seventy years to touch—
mist and peace dwell here.

—SHIEMAN

Abstractions such as love and peace, as mentioned in these haiku, might better be implied by the name of some object or season word which would give the tone.

It may be concluded that a season word, or at least a season feeling, if not strictly necessary, is at least desirable for broadening the scope of haiku. Since each season has certain aspects of nature which seem proper to it alone, conventions similar to the formulae of oral poetry traditions have grown up. The season word usually contributes to the tone of a poem by providing comparison or contrast with another image. In addition, it often adds to the melancholy effect of poems dealing with death, sickness or loneliness. There is, therefore, little doubt that retaining the season word, or at least the season mood, is a valuable help in increasing the power of resonance of haiku, since the word brings with it the whole panorama of the time of year and its accompanying emotional responses.

VI | HAIKU TECHNIQUES

As was pointed out in Chapter 4, the simple diction of haiku illustrates the Zen love of the ordinary. It is one of the purposes of this chapter to show how the Japanese love for simple, everyday things extends to the choice of words for haiku. Related to the use of vocabulary in both Japanese and English haiku is the effective employment of poetic techniques, as will be seen in an examination of natural imagery, assonance and alliteration, verbal dexterity, allusion, enjambment, rhythm and rhyme. In addition, it will be noted that in English haiku a further development, anthropomorphism, occurs. To some extent, the remarks which Earl Miner makes about *waka* may be applied to haiku. In "Techniques in Japanese Poetry," Miner discusses the five-line poems from the point of view of imagery, alliteration and assonance, generalization, allegory and verbal dexterity. Many of his insights regarding *waka* apply equally to haiku, although those on allegory and generalization, on the whole, do not.[1]

SIMPLE DICTION

The most remarkable thing about Japanese haiku is, perhaps, their simple diction. This is best illustrated by the common, everyday vocabulary (recalling Wordsworth's "selection" of ordinary words) used in haiku by Basho.

> *Samidare wo*
> *Atsumete hayashi*
> *Mogami-gawa*
>
> Collecting all
> The rains of May
> The swift Mogami River.

May rains, collected, swift, Mogami River—these are the four simple words used in this haiku, which is much more beautiful in Japanese than in English. *Samidare* (May rains or June rains, depending on our calendar) has a soft, calm sound like the actual rain of the season, since the *a*'s are pronounced "ah," the final *e* is also pronounced and all the syllables have equal stress. *Atsumete hayashi* (gathering swift), in the second line, contrasts with the calm of *samidare* in the first, both in meaning and in sound. Mogami-gawa is a place name, the literal meaning of the Japanese characters for the words *mo* and *kami* being "most high" or "upper-

most," possibly either because the Mogami rushes
from the highest mountain in the district or because it
is the river flowing from the highest source on a cer-
tain mountain. Undoubtedly the simple diction of this
haiku is typical of Japanese haiku in general.

English haiku writers also, on the whole, choose
ordinary words. The best writers, realizing that Japa-
nese haiku contain five or six words at most, strengthen
the impact of their work by compression.

> A bitter morning:
> sparrows sitting together
> without any necks.
>
> —HACKETT

Bitter, morning, sparrow, sit, neck—this diction is
simple, strong Anglo-Saxon, with disyllables which
are excellent for filling out the 17 syllables in a breath-
length. A reading of many English haiku reveals that
those which use ordinary, natural diction are generally
the most effective.

NATURAL IMAGERY

In haiku, the natural image is itself an adequate
symbol. In Basho's Mogami River haiku, for example,
the phrase "the rains of May" conjures up a definite
image for the Japanese reader. Everyone knows, this
reader would tell the Westerner, that the May rains

are very beautiful but also very sad. As Miner observed in the context of *waka* poetry, the use of this type of phrase "is not so much a device as an observed fact." The May rains contain within themselves

> a traditional value or meaning which is redefined and restated in the context of each new poem. . . . "Natural imagery" is probably the best term for this metaphorical language, since the poets write from observation of nature and from a centuries-old poetic and religious tradition of mingled Buddhism, animism and Taoism.[2]

The following poems contain a simple expression of experience with, perhaps, the contrast between the stability of land and the motion of the sea brought into clearer focus by a third image. The first poem is by Basho.

> *Araumi ya*
> *Sado ni yokoto*
> *Ama-no gawa*

> A wild sea:
> And the Galaxy stretching out
> Over the island of Sado.

The stability of the island of Sado is contrasted with

the wild movement of the sea, the two images being united by the path of stars.

> These Pacific waves—
> touching how many countries
> and the child's feet?
>
> —CHENOWETH

The countries of the world, in their stability, are contrasted with the waves in their mobility, and both are united by the image of a child's feet touching part of them.

Sometimes, too, as in this poem by Basho, natural imagery is used to express the speaker's emotion.

> *Futari mishi*
> *Yuki wa kotoshi mo*
> *Furikeru ka.*

> The snow we saw come down,—
> Has it fallen,
> This year too?

The poet, lonesome for his friend, recalls the winter before, when together they had watched the snow falling. The delicate expression of affection implies that the snow fell especially for them, and therefore he doubts that it can fall when they are apart.

Footsteps echoing
through the city's canyoned walls—
faceless strangers pass.

—VIOLET PARKS

The imagery of echoing footsteps and faceless strangers suggests the loneliness of the writer.

Furthermore, at times nature seems to be out of harmony with itself, as in this poem by Basho.

Kashinoki no
Hana ni kamawanu
Sugata kana

The oak tree
Regardless of the cherry
Stands in majesty.

But what seems to be disharmony in nature is really only the human observer projecting his own disharmony onto the natural scene. To him, the oak tree is "disregarding" the cherry; but the oak tree has no such thought in mind. Poems like this one, says Miner "deal with the relation of the speaker of the poem *to the rest of nature*. What is apparently out of place in the natural order is really out of place in man. Appearance and reality; man out of step with nature which includes him."[3] The poet, seeming to tell us only about nature, has also told us something about himself. A similar relation can be seen in a poem by an American.

> The sea's voice lifting
> defiantly calling out—
> the same voice answers.
>
> —PARKS

Here again it is actually the human observer who is defiant, not the sea.

It is possible to use natural imagery to advantage in English, yet in its use there are three chief hazards: dulling the image by abstraction, explaining the image and anthropomorphism. Ezra Pound, in *Poetry*, March, 1913, advises the poet against using a single word which is not absolutely necessary, a precept he may have learned from haiku. He warns that such expressions as "dim lands of peace" dull the image by mixing "an abstraction with the concrete." This is a result of the writer's "not realizing that the natural object is always the *adequate* symbol."[4]

Pound, realizing that even those who cannot understand a symbol can understand the poetic quality of a passage, likes to use natural imagery. For him a hawk is not an ornament but simply a hawk. For poets accustomed to such abstractions as "big business," "chill Penury," and "Progress," it is difficult to keep the natural image free from abstraction.

> Machines uprooted
> blossoming apricot trees.
> Progress never weeps.
>
> —CHENOWETH

In the last line the poet is saying in a clever way that she is weeping. But would it not be clearer merely to say that she is weeping and thus to imply that Progress, indicated anyway by the machines, never weeps?

The second hazard, explaining the image, is illustrated by the same verse. The juxtaposed images of the machine and the tree need no further explanation than the brief statement of the scene, unless it be a binding image such as sound or enveloping sunshine.

The third hazard, perhaps the most prevalent, is anthropomorphism.

> With slender fingers
> the morning sun probes shadows
> discovers two deer.
>
> —MOLLY GARLING[5]

For some reason, writers of haiku in English give hands, feet, eyes, ears to natural objects. Examples could be multiplied of flowers hesitating, teasing, shouting or listening with bated breath, of the sun walking or of stars being born. The tradition in English poetry of attributing human faculties to inanimate things may be acceptable in a longer poem, and even occasionally in haiku. However, its abuse leads to a coy, cloying type of verse which militates against the serious acceptance of English haiku. In the example, the "slender fingers" of the sun might be acceptable if the ellipsis were not unnatural in the expression "probes shadows / discovers." Thus, anthropomorphism, along with overexplanation and abstraction, are generally suspect in haiku.

ASSONANCE, ALLITERATION AND ONOMATOPOEIA

The Japanese language favours assonance and alliteration because in Japanese every consonant sound (except, at times, *n*) is, without fail, accompanied by a vowel. This is illustrated by the phonetic alphabet, which begins *a i u e o ka ki ku ke ko sa shi su se so,* and goes on to make 46 syllables. Hence, it is evident that the language is highly assonant.

Geoffrey Bownas states that the sound of the letter *o* generally gives an effect of dullness, obscurity and profundity; *a* denotes clarity and splendour, *k* melancholy, *s* softness and tenderness and *h* a suggestion of bloom or expansion.[6] The French poet Rimbaud also found peculiar significance in certain sounds. His poem entitled "Voyelles" begins, "A noir, E blanc . . ." For him *a* is black, *e* is white, *i* is red, *u* is green, and *o* is blue. Other poets may disagree with Rimbaud's analysis of the "personalities" of the vowel sounds, but no one will deny the necessity of studying sounds.

The accents being almost equal throughout, Japanese speech has a cadenced harmony comparable to liturgical chant, as Joseph Yamagiwa has remarked.[7]

Basho's Mogami River haiku illustrates the advantages of the language.

> *Samidare wo*
> *Atsumete hayashi*
> *Mogami-gawa*

The many "ah" and "oh" sounds coupled with the *s*, *ts* and *sh* sounds in the second line faithfully echo the sense of the water heard rushing down the mountain, as contrasted with the soft sound of fine rain falling in the first line; the last line with its gentle nasal *g* sounds (the first one slightly nasal like the *g* in "sing") has a euphony which expresses the tender melancholy feeling evoked by the place name. Parenthetically, it might be remarked that Japanese place names are permeated with emotions associated with the whole history and atmosphere of each area, very much as Stonehenge and Montmartre are in Europe. (At the risk of digressing, it might also be noted that North American place-names provide a rich and largely untouched source of haiku polysyllabics. Such assonant and allusive Spanish and Indian names as Ottawa, Mississippi, Hochelaga, Abitibi, Caughnawaga, San Francisco, Los Angeles; French and Eskimo names like Qu'Appell, Lac à l'Eau Jaune, Adlavik; colourful names like Medicine Hat, Main Topsail, Confusion Bay, Witless Bay, Blockhead Bay, Joe Batt's Arm, Seldom, Crowsnest Pass and Cut Knife—all might be eminently suitable for haiku or *senryu*.)

Since there is little rhythmic accent in Japanese, and few pauses between the words of haiku, alliteration becomes synonomous with consonance and assonance. However, it is not difficult to find haiku, like this by Hagi-jo, with visual as well as oral alliteration.

> *Kasa torete*
> *Ame muzan naru*
> *Kakashi kana*
>
> His *kasa* fallen off
> The rain beats down pitilessly
> On the scarecrow.

The repeated "ka" sounds echo the sense of the rain beating a merciless tattoo on the scarecrow, who has lost his hat (*kasa*). The structure of the Japanese language makes for a lightness of sound which English haiku writers would do well to emulate. To be generally avoided is the heaviness of the following:

The praying mantis
betrays the twig of the tree.
Late frost blackens buds.

—CHENOWETH

The many consonant clusters make this verse much
longer than the one breath required by either haiku
custom or by the meaning.

Assonance and alliteration are used in English haiku,
as in other English poetry forms, for added depth of
meaning and as a binding, unifying element.

Seedlings in the ground
and snows from the Sierra
in my sprinkling can.

—TASHJIAN

Although several consonant clusters tend to weight it,
the short *i* sounds do redeem this poem. The slower
second line reflects the majesty of the Sierra mountains,
in contrast to the fragility of the seedlings and the
fluidity of the water in the sprinkling can. The *s*
sounds are a unifying element. Thus, from this and
other examples which could be quoted, it may be seen
that assonance and alliteration are important techniques
in English as in Japanese haiku.

Contributing to the charm and music of the Japa-
nese language are innumerable repetitious and ono-
matopoeic words such as *perapera* (fluently), *pikapika*

(shiny), *pachipachi* (crackling), *pakapaka* (galloping), *parapara* (patter), *wakuwaku* (nervously), *tsurutsuru* (slippery)—all of which are used to great advantage in haiku.

> *Uma hokuhoku*
> *Ware wo e ni miru*
> *Natsu-no kana*

> I find myself in a picture
> The cob ambles slowly
> Across the summer moor.

Hokuhoku (ambling) reinforces the mood of the summer scene in this poem by Basho.

English also is rich in onomatopoeic words which, although they may be less musically repetitive, are stronger than the Japanese words.

> The farmer hears news
> of future crops, the dot-dash
> sound of rain patter.
>
> —CHENOWETH

"Dot-dash" is much stronger and less trite than would be "the pitter-patter of raindrops," and the use of "patter" as the final noun in a less usual expression is quite effective.

South-bound roaring past
splintering the night with sound—
listen! a cricket.

—ANNE RUTHERFORD

In addition to the strong onomatopoeic word "roar,"
the many s sounds echo the sense of the train heard
in unison with the cricket. Haiku benefits from ono-
matopoeia judiciously used. As A. F. Scott writes, "in
poetry the meaning of words lies in their sound as
much as in their sense."[8]

KIREJI, MAKURA-KOTOBA AND KAKE-KOTOBA

Three further technical words often used in connec-
tion with Japanese poetry are *kireji* (cutting-word),
makura-kotoba (pillow-word) and *kake-kotoba* (pivot-
word). *Kireji,* as the name implies, are used to "cut"
the poem, that is, to indicate a pause or a final stop.
The two chief cutting-words in Japanese are *ya* and
kana. *Ya* often indicates a pause, as Harold G. Hender-
son writes. It "divides a haiku into two parts and is
usually followed by a description or comparison,
sometimes by an illustration of the feeling evoked.
There is always at least the suggestion of a kind of
equation, so that the effect of *ya* is often best indicated
by a colon."[9] Basho's frog poem contains this particle

in the first line: *"Furuike ya"* (An old pond). *Kana* is usually employed to mark the end of a haiku; in addition, "it has an indefinable emotional effect, sometimes like that of a soft sigh"[10] or an "Ah!" or "Oh!" giving emphasis to the word preceding it, as in the scarecrow poem quoted above, where the last line is: *"Kakashi kana"* (The scarecrow). *Kireji* are also mild exclamations, which, according to Joseph K. Yamagiwa, "are the chagrin of the translator who can usually come up with nothing more than a series of monotonous 'ohs' and 'ahs' and a few exclamation points."[11]

Cutting-words may have their origin in the fact that there are no punctuation marks in traditional Japanese, and quotation marks and other Western punctuation have only recently come into vogue in longer writing. Even now, punctuation is not generally used in haiku; in its stead the cutting-word is still in use. Thus it would seem that English punctuation, with its fine nuances, would adequately substitute for *kireji*. An examination of the shades of meaning indicated by the semicolon, the colon, the linking dash, the exclamation mark and suspension points reveals their value in haiku. Harold Whitehall clarifies the meaning of the various symbols:

> The semicolon (;), colon (:), and dash (—) are symbolic conjunctions capable of linking subject-predicate constructions without need of conjunc-

tions proper. They differ chiefly in the way they direct emphasis. Semicolons distribute it more or less equally between preceding and following statements. . . . The colon is used when emphasis is to be thrown forward upon the word-group or word that follows it. . . . The dash is . . . to be used when the word-group or word following it is considered to be subsidiary to, a reinforcement or example of, or an unexpected addition to what precedes it. It directs the reader's attention backward.[12]

The semicolon, colon and dash are no doubt the three most useful linking symbols for haiku. Of the separating punctuation marks, the period, indicating a full stop, "separates sentences only. The exclamation mark (!) and the question mark (?), normally used to separate special types of sentences, are also used occasionally to separate parts of sentences."[13] However, the comma separates parts of sentences only. The question mark and the exclamation point have some emotional impact, in that the question mark reverberates by calling for an answer, and the exclamation point is used "when an utterance is surcharged with emotion."[14] These two in particular are meaningful in haiku when judiciously used. In addition, suspension points (triple periods or dots) which indicate a more or less extensive omission "are often used to indicate omissions deliberately left to the reader's imagination."[15] Since this challenge of the reader's imagination is, as has been noted, a characteristic of haiku, suspension points should find a place in the English forms. It must be remembered, however, that, as restraint is a keynote of haiku, all punctuation, like *kireji,* is more meaningful if used sparingly.

If *kireji* may be said to correspond to English punctuation, the *makura-kotoba* (pillow-word) may be classified as an adjective which has evolved in the poetic tradition to describe certain other words. It is used partly for its rhythmical value, partly for its connotations,[16] very much like the Old English kennings. An example of *makura-kotoba* is *kusa-makura* (grass-pillow), which in time came to modify *tabi* (journey). This technique should be used with caution, for it calls for great artistry if triteness is to be avoided. The word "henpecked," related exclusively to "husband," might be a good example of a pillow-word in modern English.

The *kake-kotoba* (pivot-word) is a sort of pun in which, as Yamagiwa writes, a single sequence of syllables is made to pivot from one meaning to another in the course of a sentence.[17]

> *Kome kai ni*
> *Yuki no fukuro ya*
> *Nagezukin*

> Going to buy rice
> The snow-covered bag
> As a kerchief.

Yuki, in this poem by Basho, means both "going" and "snow." The haiku is, literally: rice-buying / going-snow bag / kerchief. The use of the cutting-word *ya* to project the thought ahead is well illustrated. The pivot word is *yuki,* which performs a different syntactical function in each of the two word groups on either side of it.

Although puns are sometimes considered to be the lowest form of humour in English, no less an authority than Shakespeare can be quoted to illustrate their serious use, as Donald Keene has noted. In *Macbeth,* for instance, at a highly tragic moment in the play occur the lines:

> Your castle is surpriz'd; your wife and Babes
> Savagely slaughtered: To relate the manner
> Were on the Quarry of these murther'd Deere
> To add the death of you. (IV, iii, 239-42)

Shakespeare did not expect "Deere" to evoke laughter,[18] any more than Basho expects his *kake-kotoba* to do so. Pivot-words in English could well be syntactical, with, for example, the same noun acting as object of one verb and subject of another, as in the old ballad

"Sir Patrick Spens." There, in the lines "And sent it to Sir Patrick Spens / Was walking on the strand," the name "Sir Patrick Spens" is the object of the preposition "to" and at the same time the subject of the verb "was walking."

So far, however, this construction is rare in English and, of the three, *kireji, makura-kotoba* and *kake-kotoba,* it is perhaps the third which is the greatest single differentiating factor between Japanese and English haiku.

To be aware of the relationship of *kireji* to English punctuation and of the presence of *makura-kotoba* and *kake-kotoba* in Japanese haiku is important for writers of English haiku, who would do well to experiment with these three interesting techniques and always keep their potentialities in mind.

VERBAL DEXTERITY

Closely related to the *kake-kotoba* is a device Miner calls an

> unusual technique which can scarcely be named anything other than verbal dexterity. To call the many devices which obtain two or three meanings out of a single line mere puns or word-plays, relegates such poetry to that acrostic land to which Dryden dismissed Shadwell. The double meaning . . . enables the poet to say two things at once,

not for the sake of the shock that one series of
sounds can have two meanings, but because the
method is both economical and a way of discover-
ing truth.[19]

The custom of writing haiku in phonetic syllables
rather than in Chinese ideographs and of running the
letters together in meaningful word-groups encourages
this technique. Even now this style of brush-writing
is used wherever several meanings are found. The fol-
lowing poem by Basho exemplifies verbal dexterity.

> *Ara toto*
> *Aoba wakabano*
> *Hi no hikari*

> Ah, how glorious!
> The young leaves, the green leaves
> Glittering in the sunshine!

Although this poem seems to be a simple rejoicing in
nature, *ara toto* really means "how divine" and *hi no
hikari* has the same meaning as the place-name Nikko,
which is a great religious centre deeply loved by the
Japanese people. Basho is not only rejoicing in the
scene; he is also full of reverent awe for Tokugawa
Ieyasu, the great historical figure enshrined at Nikko.

Although there are homonyms in English which

might allow the composition of haiku having several levels of meaning, depending on the sounds of the words, yet English spelling often distinguishes the various meanings and tends to render difficult this type of verbal dexterity. On the other hand, it is possible to telescope meaning by making full use of association, as is done successfully by such poets as Yeats and Eliot. In lines from "The Waste Land" Eliot uses almost verbatim Shakespeare's famous reference to Cleopatra:

> The barge she sat in, like a burnished throne,
> Burned on the water; . . . (II, ii, 199–200)

Eliot simply changed "barge" to "Chair," "burned" to "glowed" and "water" to "marble," thus compressing the style and adding a rich train of association. There is no lack of further examples to illustrate that recent poetry in English has the discipline, the concentration and the allusive power to convey several levels of meaning at the same time. Perhaps this quality of concentration is the English equivalent to the more facile verbal dexterity of the Japanese.

ALLUSION, ENJAMBMENT, RHYME AND RHYTHM

In a previous chapter it was pointed out that the brevity of the haiku form is possible partly because it rests on a continuing tradition. One word such as "cherry" calls up a host of associations and connects the poem with hundreds of others. The brief life of the cherry blossom reminds the world that youth and innocence are short-lived. Their beauty does not consist in their present loveliness but in the concept that this beauty stands poised upon the brink of destruction. In World War II the *kamikaze* pilots were compared to cherry blossoms shining against the sky for a moment, then falling. "The poignancy of the situation, the compassion of the observer toward it, create the essentially melancholy yet pleasurable quality in Japanese thought and art which Daisetz Suzuki describes as ' "feeling" the sentiments moving in things about oneself.' "[20] Blyth's volumes on haiku give scores of further examples of allusive words in Japanese haiku.

Allusion, particularly classical allusion, has always been used to advantage in English poetry, nor is it unknown in English haiku.

> By an ancient pond
> a bullfrog sits on a rock
> waiting for Basho.
>
> —SCOTT ALEXANDER[21]

This contains obvious allusions to and echoes of Basho's haiku. The last line also recalls the title of Samuel Beckett's play, *Waiting for Godot*. Perhaps this should rightly be called a *senryu* about the folly of spending time on haiku. Keats's "Ode to a Nightingale," with its allusions to Lethe and Provence, to the Hippocrene fountain, to Bacchus and to the *Old Testament* "Story of Ruth," is one of the abounding examples of English allusive poetry. Conceivably Japanese haiku, too, will be alluded to more and more in English haiku.

Although allusion is welcome in haiku, enjambment (the run-on line) is generally to be avoided. Since, as has been noted earlier, the three lines of haiku tell the where, the when and the what of the haiku moment, enjambment in haiku seems cumbersome. In long blank-verse paragraphs run-on lines have their value, but in haiku they prove to be, on the whole, too weighty. In Japanese haiku, the traditional use of *kireji* (cutting-words) discourages enjambment.

> *Asa-tsuyu ni*
> *Yogorete suzushi*
> *Uri no doro*

> In the morning dew,
> Dirty, but fresh,
> The muddy melon.

Each line of this haiku by Basho presents a fresh concept, a fairly self-sufficient word-grouping. This is the ideal to be sought in haiku.

Dewdrops outlining
the new rose leaves, first viewed, show
asymmetrical!

—BARBARA OGDEN MORAW

The choice of polysyllabic words in the two five-syl-
lable lines is excellent, but the ponderousness of the
consonant-heavy second line is increased by the slow-
ing effect of two commas. It is true that the incom-
plete feeling of the word "show," following, as it does,
a comma, has the effect of hurrying the reader on to
the third line, and this hurrying, joined to the final
exclamation mark, contributes an air of triumph to
the conclusion. There might be some justification for
the enjambment, then, in the dramatic force it gives
to the final line. On the other hand, the sense of the
haiku does not seem to call for dramatic underlining.
The demands of *shibumi, sabi, wabi* and *aware* would,
indeed, require a little less emphasis. In general, the
frail structure of haiku cannot support enjambment,
unless in exceptional cases where the artist could handle
it in a meaningful way.

Rhyme also is usually to be avoided in haiku, as be-
ing too rich for the light form. R. H. Blyth goes so far
as to say that it is to be "avoided, even if felicitous and
accidental." On the other hand, Henderson and Yasuda
are in favour of it. An examination of translations by
these three men is enlightening.

Michinobe no
Mukuge wa uma ni
Kuware-keri

Even for one unfamiliar with the meaning, this un-rhymed, highly alliterative verse by Basho is inter-esting.

> Near the road it flowered,
> the mallow—and by my horse
> has been devoured.

> [HENDERSON]

This is an expanded translation of the first line, espe-cially, of Basho's poem, which reads literally, "the roadside," in the adjectival sense. Like many other translations by Henderson, it is lengthened, in order to support the rhyme, beyond the ordinary breath which haiku demands.

Daikon-hiki
Daikon de michi wo
Oshie keri

This particularly apt haiku by Issa describes a *daikon* picker showing the way to a stranger by pointing with his *daikon*, a vegetable which comes in many varieties, all of them white, some resembling a parsnip, some a huge turnip. "Radish" in the following translation gives to many a false picture of what Issa was saying.

> With the radish he
> Pulls out, a radish-worker
> Shows the road to me.
>
> [YASUDA]

For the sake of the rhyme, awkward run-on phrases are used. Yasuda's translation suffers by comparison with one by Blyth.

> The turnip-puller
> Points the way
> With a turnip.

Terse, keeping the key word to the last, this translation faithfully renders the mood of Issa's poem.

However, in all fairness it must be pointed out that some English haiku containing rhyme are not altogether unsuccessful. A haiku by Basho quoted earlier is translated by Blyth:

> Nothing intimates,
> In the voice of the cicada,
> How soon it will die.

This excellent translation has no need of rhyme. Yet

others have used rhyme, as Henderson did in his translation of the same poem:

> So soon to die
> and no sign of it is showing—
> locust cry.

This cannot be criticised for its rhyme. It is interesting to note that the only rhyming sound is a vowel also used in Yasuda's translation:

> In the cicada's cry
> There's no sign that can foretell
> How soon it must die.

This translation seems cumbersome, compared with Blyth's. Yet the rhyming vowels are not unpleasant; perhaps, if rhyme is to be used successfully, rhyming vowels might be chosen.

Another interesting use of vowels occurs when feminine and masculine rhymes are combined in "hermaphrodite" rhyme.

> A crimson dragonfly,
> As it lights, sways together
> With a leaf of rye.

Yasuda here employs a feminine ending in the first line,

where the primary accent is on the first syllable of "dragonfly," to rhyme with a masculine ending, "rye," in the last line. Again, the only rhyming sounds are vowels. In a haiku using only feminine rhyme, the effect is different:

> A lizard flicks over
> The undulating ripples
> Of sunlit clover.

Yasuda's choice of two rhyming syllables produces the over-heaviness criticised earlier, although the effect is somewhat lighter than when masculine rhyme is used.

Slant rhyme, since it is subtler, more delicate and less obvious, is, it seems, more suitable for haiku.

> In the setting sun
> The scarecrow's shadow leans out
> To the road alone.
>
> [YASUDA]

In this haiku by Satomura Shoha (1521–1600) "sun" and "alone" rhyme approximately, to the advantage of the poem. Repetition and internal rhyme might also be successful as approximating the Japanese onomatopoeic words, especially if the poet could succeed as well as Coleridge did in these lines from *The Ancient Mariner*:

Alone, alone, all, all alone,
Alone on a wide, wide sea!

As far as rhyme is concerned, the weaker forms, notably hermaphrodite and slant rhyme, are more effective in haiku because they are unobtrusive and delicate in contrast to masculine rhyme, which is usually too rich for the slight frame of the ideal six- or seven-word haiku.

In a largely unrhymed three-line form such as haiku the problem of rhythm does not seem to be acute. As the language is unstressed, the rhythm of Japanese haiku consists simply in the 5–7–5 arrangement. As for English haiku, the consensus of opinion seems in accord with Blyth's preference for the rhythm of free verse, "a two-three-two rhythm, but not regularly iambic or anapestic."[22] In other words, rhythm should be decided by the poet in answer to the demands of the individual haiku, and need not be inherent in the definition of the form. Yasuda speaks of "haiku measure," which is the rhythm characteristic of each line, and of "vertical" and "horizontal" rhythm. For him, vertical rhythm, or the rhythm of meter, is not so important in haiku as horizontal rhythm, the rhythm of the thought which comes at the haiku moment. His stand is that "the rhythm of the thought-flow should be the primary consideration and that vertical rhythm (i.e., stressed and unstressed syllables) should vivify and make alive the experience in the poem."[23] Meter which is definitely subordinate to thought and left to the discretion of the haiku poet seems to be most suitable for English haiku.

The diction and techniques of haiku, examined at some length above, can be summarized as follows. Simplicity of diction, as illustrated by Basho's Mogami River haiku and Hackett's sparrow poem, corresponds to the Zen love of everyday things and is an essential characteristic of haiku. Natural imagery in haiku, providing adequate symbolism in itself, is used sometimes as a simple expression of experience, sometimes to express the speaker's emotion and yet again to show nature seemingly out of harmony. The use of natural imagery in English is attended by three hazards: the tendency to dull the image by abstraction, by explaining the image and by anthropomorphism. These hazards are easily avoided by the poet who is forewarned against them. Assonance and alliteration are helpful techniques in unifying the three lines of haiku and in deepening their meaning. Onomatopoeia and allusion, particularly prevalent in both languages, are strong elements. The techniques of haiku also include cutting-words, pillow-words and pivot-words, as well as typically Japanese verbal dexterity. Experimentation with all these devices by writers of English haiku will be stimulated, it is hoped, by the explanations given here. Free-verse rhythms are considered most appropriate for haiku. Enjambment and rhyme should be avoided, as a rule, but care must be taken, if they are used, to adjust them to the needs of the delicate haiku form.

Differences in language and poetic tradition may cause varying emphases in the use of haiku techniques, but those of Japanese and English are not essentially different, as Miner has pointed out. As the poet Takahama Kyoshi (1894–1959) wrote:

> *Aki kaze ya*
> *Ganchu no mono*
> *Mina haiku.*

> Autumn wind:
> Everything I see—
> Is haiku.

[BOWNAS AND THWAITE]

The most important element of haiku—the experience of the haiku moment—is possible to poets in all cultures. The development and mastery of adequate techniques is a matter of experimentation and practice.

CONCLUSION

Like the sonnet, the haiku form has entered English letters from a foreign land. Heir to the riches of Buddhism, Taoism, Confucianism and Shinto, haiku is above all permeated with the spirit of Zen. Growing as it does from the linked-verse tradition of seventeenth-century Japan, and brought to perfection by Basho, haiku endeavours to express the Zen religious experience of enlightenment, the poetic counterpart of which is the flash of insight and union with nature called the haiku moment. Haiku partakes of the Zen qualities of directness and paradoxicality, austerity and joy, love of nature and love of ordinary actions and utensils.

The Zen qualities and the haiku form are compatible with Western religious thought and poetics. Similarly, the three-line stanza and the 17 syllables are appropriate expressions of the variety in symmetry and the unity in diversity required by the haiku intuition. Brevity is achieved and depth provided by rich allusiveness and especially by the use of the season word, which can also be used to great advantage in English haiku.

Of special importance to the haiku form are its simple diction and natural imagery. Additional techniques are of interest: alliteration, onomatopoeia, cutting-words, pillow-words, pivot-words, verbal dexterity. These techniques do not essentially differ from those of poets writing in English. The place of allusion, personification, enjambment, rhyme and rhythm are a necessary part of any study of haiku.

In the West there has been considerable general interest in haiku and an understanding, among such modern poets as Ezra Pound, of the fundamental Japanese poetic "atmosphere" of compression and natural imagery. Yet relatively few of the so-called English haiku are really haiku. It has been the purpose of this study to find out why. Two causes for the problems of writing haiku in English have been identified here— lack of understanding of the Japanese haiku form and insufficient experimentation with truly native English haiku.

Three chapters of this book have given some indication of the background of Japanese haiku; but a serious poet, in addition to studying related material in translation and in the works of English authors, would do well to learn the Japanese language in order to be able to read haiku in the original. After thus becoming imbued with the spirit of haiku and with the tonal qualities and texture of the language, the poet could advance to the second stage, that of building up a native English haiku tradition. English haiku must not be pale imitations of Japanese haiku, or mere pseudo-Buddhist travesties. Native haiku in English must be an outcome of the poet's own experience, a rediscovery of the richness of the poet's own cultural tradition. Subjects must be native—there is no place for the cherry blossom, the *hototogisu,* the rice planter, the Buddha statue or the windbell. There is a place, however, for such typically Western subjects as apple blossoms, swallows, wheatfields, beaches, grey cathedrals, ice cubes—anything which may be an expression of the haiku moment for Western man.

As for the technicalities of English haiku, the three-line form and the season word should be retained; they belong to the essence of haiku and are equally valuable to writers of haiku in English and in Japanese. The 17 syllables should be adapted for haiku in English but, since English is an accented language, this adaptation may call for two lines of iambic dimeter, possibly having slant rhyme, separated by a line of iambic trimeter. Enjambment should probably be avoided in favour of three relatively self-contained lines. The present writers of haiku in English need to give a great deal of thought to the problem of overly long English syllables. These writers should experiment more with polysyllabic and quickly articulated words. Increased attention should be directed to allusion and to onomatopoeia, assonance, consonance and slant rhyme. Most of these are used to great advantage in Japanese haiku and are valuable in English also. (One can envision a whole group of allusive English haiku beginning "O wind, . . .") A campaign should be begun to rid English haiku of sentimentality and especially of anthropomorphism. Perhaps because of the freshness, delicacy and brevity of the haiku form, there has been great danger of allowing the English haiku to degenerate into this debilitating form of sentimentality.

Two areas for investigation and experimentation are punctuation (not native to the Japanese language but meaningful in English) and tone. English haiku cannot be as melancholy as the Japanese, because the Western poetic tradition usually prefers a more vigorous approach. Nevertheless, an awareness and appreciation of the meaning and advantages of *sabi, shibumi* and similar aesthetic qualities cannot but improve the climate for haiku in English. When the meaning and techniques of Japanese haiku have been studied in depth, similar study and thought must be given to English haiku. Fortunately, students of today are being introduced to haiku early. With these students' growing interest in poetics and textual criticism, their revolt against excessive pragmatism and materialism and their enthusiasm for simplicity and self-dedication, every possibility exists for the emergence of a great haiku poet who will take the Japanese form and give it the truly English shape that is waiting for it.

The ostensibly simple, swiftly pronounceable words of haiku in English should hold a depth of meaning—a meaning which will embody the spirit of the newly naturalized form. This spirit might well consist of an existential search for the essences of things and an effort to re-unite the fragmented parts of man's consciousness. But English haiku will be nothing more than a parlour game, or a device used by teachers to introduce children to poetry, until it is allied to the best of Western culture and becomes one of its native forms, having a spirit of its own that is similar to, yet actually quite different from, that of the Japanese haiku.

If the haiku form is to be assimilated in this way, poets must realize its depth and expressive possibilities. To do this, it must be repeated, they should seek a thorough knowledge of the Japanese language and of Japanese culture and poetics. With knowledge of haiku spread throughout the world, one might well expect a broadening and enriching of this form comparable to the Renaissance sonnet's expansion and deepening, once it spread beyond the Alps.

The basic problem facing an English haiku poet is, of course, to determine to what extent the Japanese form should be followed. This answer, it is hoped, has been made clear during the course of this work—that haiku is not haiku unless it expresses a haiku moment, contains a season word and approximately 17 syllables in three lines usually divided into 5, 7, and 5 syllables. Too often poets, content to adopt the techniques without understanding them, have written pseudo-haiku. To readers with insufficient knowledge, these are apparently very Japanese; to one who knows real haiku, they fail on three chief counts.

In the first place, there is usually a strained and deliberate attempt to be profoundly philosophical. The successful use of cryptic comment by modern cerebral poets influences these writers in their desire to be profound, to write in the line of the philosopher poets, to associate poetry with deep thought. The solutions to the problem of over-cerebration in haiku are, first, to remember that the natural image itself is an adequate symbol and, second, to read good haiku. Then poets will avoid writing haiku like this:

> Leave fallow a small
> corner of this field, son,
> some seeds of thought have wings.
>
> —JOY SHIEMAN

and recognize the value of this by Basho:

> *Shiho yori*

Hana fuki-irete
Nio no umi

From all directions
Come cherry petals
Blowing into the lake of Nio.

The first poem, good by Western standards, is too pretentiously cerebral. Basho's says as much while remaining faithful to the haiku moment.

The second outstanding fault of English haiku is coyness and anthropomorphism, a preoccupation with making things speak instead of letting them speak. The solution to this problem is to state without comment. Not

White calla lilies—
you can surely tease a croak
from this plastic frog.

—TASHJIAN

but the following by Buson:

Byakuren wo
Kiran to zo omou
So no sama

A white lotus;
The monk
Is deciding to cut it.

Buson's simple statement of what he sees is much more powerful than the thoughts of the first poem.

The last of the three chief problems of writing English haiku is mistaken adaptation and slavish imitation, degenerating into unnatural ellipsis, trite season-words and meretricious adoption of Japanese things not experienced. Consider the following verse by Barbara Ogden Moraw:

> Water spirit pleased
> with spread blossoms—house spirit
> appeased with rice cake.

What has English haiku to do with house and water spirits, rice cakes and the sort of Japanese-English language produced by the unnatural ellipsis in these lines? (Note, however, the excellent use of the words "pleased" and "appeased.")

The first problem (over-cerebration) deals generally with the spirit of haiku, and the last two (anthropomorphism and slavish imitation) with the techniques. The general solution to all the problems is to become more familiar with real haiku, much as Sir Thomas Wyatt and the earl of Surrey did with the sonnet when they translated it, and as Milton did when he wrote five sonnets in Italian. This grappling with the foreign form was necessary before the sonnet could be naturalized. Similarly, the background and techniques of Japanese haiku must be studied, and (as has been done by many poets on the United States West Coast) the Japanese language must be learned. Poets must develop haiku awareness. In addition, continued serious experimentation with haiku in English will help to evolve a form which, while resembling the Japanese haiku, is yet perfectly suited to the spirit, cultural traditions and idiom of English. A Surrey of haiku or an English Basho may emerge to bring the form to perfection in this language. In an age when most cultivated people wrote poetry, it took a generation for the English sonnet to become acclimatized. In the relatively non-poetic milieu of the present, we cannot expect a great writer of English haiku to come forward in a shorter period of time. Nevertheless, if the present enthusiasm continues, helped by the translators of Japanese articles on haiku and by Japanese writers of haiku, the emergence of a successful body of haiku in English should not be too far away. In effect, the future of haiku in English depends on practice, perseverance, a critical spirit—all in keeping with the Japanese artistic dictum, "Learn the rules and then throw away the book."

NOTES

CHAPTER ONE

1. Most of the information in this chapter is based on notes by Miyazaki Toshiko, a teacher of Japanese literature in Kitakyushu, Japan.

2. R. H. Blyth, *A History of Haiku* (2 vols.; Tokyo: Hokuseido, 1963–64), II, p. 195. (Hereinafter referred to as *History*.)

3. Geoffrey Bownas and Anthony Thwaite (trans.), *The Penguin Book of Japanese Verse* (Hammondsworth, Middlesex: Penguin, 1964), p. lxviii. (Hereinafter referred to as *Japanese Verse*.)

CHAPTER TWO

1. W. E. Soothill (trans.), *The Lotus of the Wonderful Law*, quoted in Tsunoda Ryusaku, Wm. Theodore deBary and Donald Keene (comps.), *Sources of Japanese Tradition* (2 vols.; New York: Columbia University Press, 1958), I, p. 117.

2. *Ibid.*

3. *Ibid.*, p. 150, "Precious Key to the Secret Treasury," quoted from *Kobo Daishi Zenshu.*

4. Miyamori Asataro, *An Anthology of Haiku Ancient and*

Modern (Tokyo: Taiseido, 1932), p. 212. (Hereinafter referred to as *Anthology*.)

5. R. H. Blyth, *Haiku* (4 vols.; Tokyo, Hokuseido, 1949), I, p. 66.

6. *Ibid.*, p. 51.

7. Maurius B. Jansen, "Introduction to the History of Japan," in Bradley Smith (ed.), *Japan: A History in Art* (New York: Simon & Schuster, 1964), p. 10. (Hereinafter referred to as *Japan*.)

8. Philip Yampolsky (comp. and trans.), *The Zen Master Hakuin* (New York: Columbia University Press, 1971), p. 116.

9. Paul Reps (comp.), *Zen Flesh, Zen Bones: A Collection of Zen and Pre-Zen Writings* (Rutland, Vermont and Tokyo, Japan: Tuttle, 1957), p. 22. (Hereinafter referred to as *Zen Flesh*.)

10. Nancy Wilson Ross (comp.), *The World of Zen: An East-West Anthology* (London: Collins, 1962), p. 7.

11. Asano Nagatake, "Introduction to the Art of Japan," in Smith (ed.), *Japan* p. 14.

12. Earle Ernst, *The Kabuki Theatre* (New York: Oxford University Press, 1956), pp. 74–75.

13. Asano, "Introduction," in Smith (ed.), *Japan*, p. 16.

14. Blyth, *Haiku*, I, p. 146.

15. D. T. Suzuki, *An Introduction to Zen Buddhism* (London: Arrow Books, 1959), p. 88.

16. *Ibid.*, p. 88.

CHAPTER THREE

1. Kenneth Yasuda, *The Japanese Haiku: Its Essential Nature, History, and Possibilities in English, with Selected Examples* (Rutland, Vermont and Tokyo, Japan: Tut-

tle, 1957), p. 30. (Hereinafter referred to as *Japanese Haiku.*)

2. *Ibid.*, p. 24.

3. Yuasa Nobuyuki (trans.), *Basho: The Narrow Road to the Deep North and Other Travel Sketches* (Hammondsworth, Middlesex: Penguin, 1966). (Hereinafter referred to as *Basho.*) p. 33.

4. Yasuda, *Japanese Haiku*, p. 24.

5. Blyth, *Haiku*, I, p. 280.

6. R. H. Blyth, *Zen in English Literature and Oriental Classics* (Tokyo: Hokuseido, 1942), p. 28. (Hereinafter referred to as *Zen.*)

7. These influences are well explained in Earl Miner, *The Japanese Tradition in British and American Literature* (Princeton, N.J.: Princeton University Press, 1958), chapters III to VI. (Hereinafter referred to as *Japanese Tradition.*)

8. Otake Masaru, "Wallace Stevens no Shi to Haiku" [Haiku and the Poems of Wallace Stevens], in *Eigo Seinen* [The Rising Generation], January 1, 1966, p. 17.

9. James Hackett, *The Way of Haiku: An Anthology of Haiku Poems* (Tokyo: Japan Publications, 1969), p. 41. (All of Hackett's haiku hereinafter quoted are from this volume.)

10. Yasuda, *Japanese Haiku*, p. xiii.

11. Blyth, *Zen*, p. 126.

12. *Ibid.*, p. 264.

13. *Ibid.*, p. 352.

14. Martin Buber, *Tales of the Hasidim: The Early Masters* (New York: Schocken Books, 1961), p. 95.

15. *Ibid.*, p. 61.

16. Blyth, *Haiku*, I, p. 225.

17. Blyth, *Haiku*, II, p. ii.

18. Although ever-increasing numbers of Japanese in the cities are living in concrete *apaato* (apartment buildings), the closeness to nature is still woven into their culture.
19. Blyth, *Zen*, p. 408.
20. Blyth, *History*, II, p. 19.
21. Alan Watts, "Haiku," edited transcript of a talk given over station KPFA-FM in Berkeley, California. Now available on an LP record, "Haiku," from Musical Engineering Associates, Box 303, Sausalito, California. Quoted by Ross, *World of Zen*, p. 123.
22. Henry S. Canby (ed.), *The Works of Thoreau* (Boston: Houghton Mifflin, 1937), pp. 272–74.
23. Reps, *Zen Flesh*, p. 36.

CHAPTER FOUR

1. Yasuda, *Japanese Haiku*, p. 31.
2. *Ibid.*, p. 31.
3. *Ibid.*, p. 33.
4. Blyth, *History*, II, p. 350.
5. Mario Pei, *The Story of Language* (Philadelphia and New York: Lippincott, 1949), p. 379.
6. *Ibid.*, p. 109.
7. Yasuda, *Japanese Haiku*, p. 34.
8. Harold G. Henderson, *Haiku in English* (Rutland, Vermont and Tokyo, Japan: Tuttle, 1967), p. 31. (Hereinafter referred to as *English*.)
9. Blyth, *History*, II, p. 350.
10. Hyder Rollins and Herschel Baker, *The Renaissance in England* (Boston: D. C. Heath, 1954), p. 656.
11. Henderson, *English*, pp. 14–15.
12. Yasuda, *Japanese Haiku*, p. 62.
13. Penny Scribner, "Haiku Poetry," in *Arts and Activities:*

The Teacher's Arts and Crafts Guide (September, 1967), pp. 46–49.

14. Miyamori, *Anthology*, p. 7.
15. Joseph K. Yamagiwa, "Literature and Japanese Culture," in J. W. Hall and R. K. Beardsley (eds.), *Twelve Doors to Japan* (New York: McGraw-Hill, 1965), p. 65. (Hereinafter referred to as *Twelve Doors*.)
16. Yasuda, *Japanese Haiku*, p. 65.
17. Scribner, "Haiku Poetry," p. 46.
18. Quoted in Henderson, *English*, p. 65.
19. Earl Miner, "The Techniques of Japanese Poetry," *Hudson Review* VIII (Autumn, 1955), p. 352.
20. Yuasa, *Basho*, pp. 48–49.
21. Louis Untermeyer (comp.), *Modern American Poetry and Modern British Poetry* (New York: Harcourt Brace Jovanovich, 1950).
22. Henderson, *English*, p. 29.
23. Blyth, *History*, II, p. 351.

CHAPTER FIVE

1. Yasuda, *Japanese Haiku*, p. 176.
2. Peter Beilenson, *Japanese Haiku* (Mount Vernon, N. Y.: Peter Pauper Press, 1956), p. 3.
3. Donald Keene, *Japanese Literature: An Introduction for Western Readers* (New York: Grove Press, 1956), p. 40. (Hereinafter referred to as *Japanese Literature*.)
4. Blyth, *Haiku*, II, p. 2.
5. Los Altos Writers Roundtable, *Borrowed Water: A Book of American Haiku* (Rutland, Vermont and Tokyo, Japan: Tuttle, 1966), p. 89. (All English haiku hereinafter quoted, except those by James Hackett, are from this volume unless otherwise indicated.)
6. Blyth, *Haiku*, II, p. 30.

7. *Ibid.*, II, p. 30.
8. *Ibid.*, III, p. 2.
9. *Ibid.*, III, p. 324.
10. *Ibid.*, III, p. 324.
11. *Ibid.*, IV, p. 164.
12. *Ibid.*, IV, p. 164.
13. Henry Goodman (ed.), *The Selected Writings of Lafcadio Hearn* (New York: Citadel Press, 1949), p. 446.

CHAPTER SIX
1. Miner, "The Techniques of Japanese Poetry," *Hudson Review* VIII (Autumn, 1955).
2. *Ibid.*, p. 353.
3. *Ibid.*, p. 355.
4. Quoted in Miner, *Japanese Tradition*, p. 123.
5. Leroy Kanterman (ed.), *Haiku West* I, No. 2 (January, 1968), p. 33.
6. Bownas and Thwaite (trans.), *Japanese Verse*, pp. lii–liii.
7. Yamagiwa, "Literature and Japanese Culture," in Hall and Beardsley (eds.), *Twelve Doors*, p. 235.
8. A. F. Scott, *The Poet's Craft* (New York: Cambridge University Press, 1957), p. x.
9. Harold G. Henderson, *An Introduction to Haiku* (Garden City, N. Y.: Doubleday, 1958), p. 189.
10. *Ibid.*, p. 187.
11. Yamagiwa, "Literature and Japanese Culture," in Hall and Beardsley (eds.), *Twelve Doors*, p. 235.
12. Harold Whitehall, *Structural Essentials of English* (New York: Harcourt Brace Jovanovich, 1956), pp. 119–35.
13. *Ibid.*, p. 124.
14. *Ibid.*, p. 126.
15. *Ibid.*, p. 132.

16. Yamagiwa, "Literature and Japanese Culture," in Hall and Beardsley (eds.), *Twelve Doors*, p. 241.
17. *Ibid.*, p. 242.
18. Keene, *Japanese Literature*, p. 5.
19. Miner, "The Techniques of Japanese Poetry," *Hudson Review* VIII (Autumn, 1955), p. 357.
20. Ernst, *Kabuki Theatre*, p. 87.
21. *Haiku West* I, No. 1 (June, 1967), p. 13.
22. Blyth, *History*, II, p. 351.
23. Yasuda, *Japanese Haiku*, p. 81.

✤ | ANNOTATED
BIBLIOGRAPHY

BOOKS

Beilenson, Peter. *Japanese Haiku*. Mount Vernon, New York: Peter Pauper Press, 1956.

> Translations of famous Japanese haiku with a good introduction.

Blyth, R. H. *Haiku*. Vol I: *Eastern Culture*. Vol. II: *Spring*. Vol III: *Summer-Autumn*. Vol. IV: *Autumn-Winter*.
Tokyo: Hokuseido, 1949–1952.

> Volume I describes the spiritual origins of haiku in Buddhism, Zen and other Oriental religions; it shows how certain verses in the great English poets are haiku. A brief section gives the techniques of haiku. Volumes II to IV analyse the chief words and concepts used to denote the seasons in haiku.

———. *A History of Haiku*. 2 vols. Tokyo: Hokuseido, 1963–64.

> Volume I gives a comprehensive history of haiku from the beginning to Issa; volume II from Issa to the present.

———. *Zen in English Literature and Oriental Classics.* Tokyo: Hokuseido, 1942.

> Illustrates principles of Zen in both English and Oriental writings. Excellent insights, but of uneven value.

Bownas, Geoffrey and Thwaite, Anthony (trans.). *The*

Penguin Book of Japanese Verse. Hammondsworth, Middlesex: Penguin, 1964.

> All types of Japanese verse from primitive times to the present. The introduction gives a brief résumé of Japanese prosody.

Canby, Henry S. (ed.). *The Works of Thoreau*. Boston: Houghton Mifflin, 1937.

Ernst, Earle. *The Kabuki Theatre*. New York: Oxford University Press, 1956.

Goodman, Henry (ed.). *The Selected Writings of Lafcadio Hearn*. New York: Citadel Press, 1949.

Hackett, James. *The Way of Haiku: An Anthology of Haiku Poems*. Tokyo: Japan Publications, 1969.

Hall, J. W. and Beardsley, R. K. *Twelve Doors to Japan*. New York: McGraw-Hill, 1965.

> Contains an excellent essay on Japanese literature by Joseph K. Yamagiwa.

Henderson, Harold G. *Haiku in English*. Rutland, Vermont and Tokyo, Japan: Tuttle, 1967.

> A brief work written in a popular style. Contains excellent insights on English haiku.

―――. *An Introduction to Haiku*. Garden City, New York: Doubleday and Company, Inc., 1958.

> Translations of well-known Japanese haiku, perceptive commentaries integrated with a history of haiku and an excellent appendix on Japanese particles.

Keene, Donald. *Japanese Literature: An Introduction for Western Readers*. New York: Grove Press, 1956.

> An excellent introduction to Japanese literature which corrects false impressions of Japanese literature and language and gives an overview of the characteristics of Japanese poetry.

Los Altos Writers Roundtable. *Borrowed Water: A Book of American Haiku*. Rutland, Vermont and Tokyo, Japan: Tuttle, 1966.

An important experiment in writing haiku which are not Japanese but truly American, dealing with Western subjects.

Miner, Earl. *The Japanese Tradition in British and American Literature*. Princeton, New Jersey: Princeton University Press, 1958.

A scholarly, well-written exposition of the influence of Japan on British and American Literature from the Renaissance to Pound and Yeats. Of particular interest is the effect of the haiku on Pound's poetry.

Miyamori Asataro. *An Anthology of Haiku Ancient and Modern*. Tokyo: Taiseido, 1932.

Haiku in Japanese, romanized Japanese and English translation, with many explanations of individual haiku, a brief comparison of haiku and epigrams, a history of haiku and sketches of four masters of haiku.

Pei, Mario. *The Story of Language*. Philadelphia: Lippincott, 1949.

Contains a brief but interesting comparison of the English and Japanese languages.

Reps, Paul (comp.). *Zen Flesh, Zen Bones: A Collection of Zen and Pre-Zen Writings*. Rutland, Vermont and Tokyo, Japan: Tuttle, 1957.

Translations of Zen stories and anecdotes.

Rollins, Hyder and Baker, Herschel. *The Renaissance in England*. Boston: D. C. Heath, 1954.

Ross, Nancy Wilson (comp.). *The World of Zen: An East-West Anthology*. London: Collins, 1962.

Contains Zen writings and a good introduction describing Zen.

Scott, A. F. *The Poet's Craft*. New York: Cambridge University Press, 1957.

Smith, Bradley (ed.). *Japan: A History in Art*. New York: Simon & Schuster, 1964.

The relationship between Japanese art and religious belief is well explained.

Stevens, Wallace. *The Collected Poems of Wallace Stevens.* New York: Alfred A. Knopf, 1955.

Suzuki, D. T. *An Introduction to Zen Buddhism.* London: Arrow Books, 1959.

> A conscientious account of Zen Buddhism particularly interesting for its explanation of *satori*.

Tsunoda Ryusaku, deBary, Wm. Theodore and Keene, Donald (comps.). *Sources of Japanese Tradition.* 2 vols. New York: Columbia University Press, 1958.

> Translations of Japanese writings, chiefly of historical, religious and literary interest, with excellent essays and commentaries.

Whitehall, Harold. *Structural Essentials of English.* New York: Harcourt Brace Jovanovich, 1956.

Yasuda, Kenneth. *The Japanese Haiku: Its Essential Nature, History, and Possibilities in English.* Rutland, Vermont and Tokyo, Japan: Tuttle, 1957.

> Provides an exhaustive study of the place of haiku in the world of literature.

Yuasa Nobuyuki (trans.). *Basho: The Narrow Road to the Deep North and Other Travel Sketches.* Hammondsworth, Middlesex: Penguin, 1966.

> Basho's most important works. The settings of his most famous poems described by the poet.

ARTICLES AND ESSAYS

Asano Nagatake. "Introduction to the Art of Japan." In Smith, Bradley (ed.). *Japan: A History in Art.* New York: Simon & Schuster, 1964.

Jansen, Maurius B. "Introduction to the History of Japan." In Smith, Bradley (ed.). *Japan: A History in Art.* New York: Simon & Schuster, 1964.

Kanterman, Leroy. *Haiku West*. New York: By the author. Nos. 1 and 2 (June, 1967 and January, 1968).

A "little magazine" containing haiku of all degrees of value and short articles about haiku.

Miner, Earl. "The Techniques of Japanese Poetry." In *Hudson Review* VIII (Autumn, 1955), 350–66.

Shows how *waka* illustrate the inner workings of Japanese poetic technique and the assumptions about life and poetry necessary to appreciate the peculiar accomplishment of Japanese lyric poetry.

Miyazaki Toshiko. "Haiku." 1965, handwritten.

Gives a brief history of haiku and criticisms of a few well-known haiku.

Otake Masaru. "Wallace Stevens no Shi to Haiku" [Haiku and the Poems of Wallace Stevens]. In *Eigo Seinen* [The Rising Generation], January 1, 1966.

Shows the haiku elements in Stevens's "Thirteen Ways of Looking at a Blackbird."

Scribner, Penny. "Haiku Poetry." In *Arts and Activities: The Teacher's Arts and Crafts Guide*, September, 1967.

Although the comments on haiku are rather superficial, there are good insights into haiku from the point of view of painting.

Yamagiwa, Joseph K. "Literature and Japanese Culture." In Hall, J. W. and Beardsley, R. K. (eds.). *Twelve Doors to Japan*. New York: McGraw-Hill, 1965.

INDEX